Analysis of Poetic Thinking

Wayne State University Press Detroit 1969

Analysis of Poetic Thinking

by Max Rieser

translated by Herbert M. Schueller

Criticism Monograph 1

Contents

Translator's Preface

I cannot remember precisely when I first met Max Rieser. It was sometime before August, 1960, when the Fourth International Congress for Aesthetics took place in Athens. During the congress, at which he gave a major address, we saw each other frequently, and thereafter we met many times at meetings of the American Society for Aesthetics, meetings at which he gave a number of papers, especially on Polish philosophy and aesthetics, a subject in which he was more knowledgeable than anyone else in the group, and perhaps more than anyone else in America.

This is not to define the limits of Rieser's subject-matter, however. His preoccupations have always been both philosophical and historical. His bibliography is long and his "outlets" are varied: *Journal of Aesthetics and Art Criticism, Journal of the History of Ideas, Journal of Philosophy,* and *Philosophical Review,* not to mention journals and newspapers of Germany, Austria, France, Switzerland, and Italy.

Early in the summer of 1963, Rieser sent me for my reading pleasure his *Analyse des Poetischen Denkens,* a monograph published in Vienna in 1954. I delayed reading it until I went on vacation. Long evenings in motels located beyond the goods and evils of civilization must be filled, and for me non-English books arousing the cross-word puzzle instinct fill them ideally. Almost automatically, I began to translate the *Analyse.* In the moments—and even years—that followed, the work proceeded in an almost leisurely fashion. I completed sections and sent them to Rieser for his advice and correction, and thus the entire monograph gradually took form in English.

This pursuit was somewhat due to my own constant fascination with how any argument couched in non-English terms can be transferred into English, but in larger part to my absorption in the development of Rieser's thesis that because poetic thinking concerns archaic emotions anterior to realistic thought, it is regressive. Here, clearly, was a work psychological and even psychoanalytical in nature which, though based on Freud's theory of the stratification of the mind, did not concentrate on single works of artists and which, in fact, contained few names. The focus was on the artistic or poetic process itself, not on persons dead or alive who wrote poems or analyses of them.

Then there was Rieser's discussion of rhythm, which reminded me of the opening of the third section of Yeats's essay, "The Symbolism of Poetry":

The purpose of rhythm, it has always seemed to me, is to prolong the moment of contemplation, the moment when we are both asleep and awake, which is the one moment of creation, by hushing us with an alluring monotony, while it holds us by variety, to keep us in that state of perhaps real trance, in which the mind liberated from the pressure of the will is unfolded in symbols. (*Essays and Introductions* [1961], p. 159)

As a philosopher, Rieser of course places in a thought-context what Yeats observed in a poetical one; yet both writers are basically psychological in stance. Rieser begins (and now I rely very largely on his own responses to my inquiries of him) by distinguishing between two languages. Like literary theorists, he calls them the languages of literature (or poetry) on the one hand and of science on the other. In the broadest of perspectives, Rieser sees the first as a classifying metrical language which in the developed stages of scientific thought is descriptively static and mathematically oriented. Its concepts are so created as to be put into definitions; and these concepts convert the world into a statistical chart in which all invariant features are enumerated and enumerable. In the prescientific stages of ordinary language, this chart is composed mainly of sentences having a copulative but not a verb—predicate—the sentence therefore being equational in form and character.

The second kind of language lists events in historical sequence and sentences, and becomes the language of history in the developed stages of science. This language has verbs as predicates. Yet it cannot ascend to calculated laws; it cannot predict; it can only relate events. Of this language the poetic is a subdivision. Being "evaluational," however, the poetic is tinged with emotive factors and tends to be regressive. It liquefies the concepts of speech into their original intuitive background components; it is saturated with musical and imagistic forms. As it sheds the conceptual frame entirely but retains visual shapes, it becomes plastic art; shedding even the particular objects, it becomes a colored surface, as in abstractions, as in the visual "abstracts" of the world.

The *Analyse* (here called *Analysis of Poetic Thinking*) therefore represents one of the focal points in the context of Rieser's conception of language as a whole. It of course is not and cannot be my purpose to make an extensive analysis of his entire position, or to compare his thesis of language with other such theories—especially as they bring science, poetry, and the arts in general into conceptual order, or to comment more specifically about his theory of poetic language. His general position can be further clarified if one reads those of Rieser's articles in English which bring his theories together. I append a short list of them. The journals in which they appear are those mentioned above, though their names are abbreviated here:

Semantics

"The Symbolic Function of Aesthetic Terms," *JAAC*, I (1941–42), 58–72; "On Musical Semantics," *JP*, XXXIX (1942), 421–32; "The Language of Shapes and Sizes in Architecture, or On Morphic Semantics," *PR*, LV (1946), 152–73; "The Semantic Theory of Art in America," *JAAC*, XV (1956–57), 12–26; "The Linguistic Theory of Plastic Art," *Atti Del III* [*1956*] *Congresso Internazionale di Estetica* (1957), 577–66; "Metaphoric Expression in the Plastic Arts," *JAAC*, XVII (1958–59), 194–200.

Art

"Brief Introduction to an Epistemology of Art," *JP*, XLVII (1950), 695–704; "The Problems of Artistic Form: The Concept of Art," *JAAC*, XXVII (1968).

Natural Beauty

"Three Principles of Natural Beauty," *JP*, LIII (1956), 354–66.

Aesthetics

"Realism and Formalism," *Rassegna di Scienze Filoso-fiche,* XVII (1964), 1–11; "Realism in Aesthetics," *Rivista di Estetica,* X (1965), 5–21.

Scientific and Poetic Thought

"Language of Poetic and Scientific Thought," *JP,* XL (1943), 421–35; "Three Stages of the Contemplation of Nature," *JP,* LII (1955), 169–81.

Beyond Science and Art

"The Function of the Notion," *PR,* LI (1942), 441–55; "On Quality, Space, and Time," *PR,* LV (1946), 534–54; "A Methodological Investigation into the Relation between Mind and Body," *JP,* XLIII (1946), 551–58; "Values of Achievement versus Values of Enjoyment," *JP,* XLIX (1952), 685–92; "The Noëtic Models of Contemporary Philosophy," *JP,* LVII (1960), 545–54; "Causation, Action, and Creation," *JP,* XXXVII (1940), 401–99.

Rieser is himself a writer of poems, a selection of which appeared in Vienna in 1967 as *Das Weltgesicht* (*The Face of the World*). He has studied the poetic process (the creation of language and of forms in language) from inside and out—from outside by imaginatively observing other poets performing the actions which are their poems, and from inside by observing himself in his own creative process. Thus the *Analysis* has some of the features of autobiography, which is probably the only firm ground there is for the description of creativity in any of the forms and types of art.

H. M. S.

1

Poetic Thinking as a Regressive Phenomenon:
The Roots of Rhythm and Sound-Symbolism

One time as I reflected on the nature of poetry, on the motives that lead the poet to his work, these words of Goethe occurred to me:

> *Ich singe, wie der Vogel singt,*
> *der in den Zweigen wohnet;*
> *Das Lied, das aus der Kehle dringt,*
> *ist Lohn, der reichlich lohnet.*

> (I sing as does the bird
> who lives in the branches;
> The song which forces its way out of the throat
> is a reward which rewards amply.)

These lines are suitable for indicating certain important basic truths: that poetry owes its existence not to an arbitrary act of the poet, but to an innate drive; that it is not the result of a decision, but that it is a natural phenomenon; that something compulsive clings to it; that it rises from an inner pressure—even though it is true also that it is not conceivable outside a social context. But it plainly shares this characteristic with language itself.

If one explains poetry primarily as a natural, instinctive kind of function of the human mind, then, as the problem is posed in this form, the task of the following investigation becomes clearer. What is to be attempted is the interpretation of a phenomenon of nature, so to speak, specifically the analysis of the art of poetry.

The aim of such an analysis is the explanation of the poetic mind, of poetic thinking. Not the themes and contents of poetic works are to be discussed and analyzed, but the poetic form. Because of the sheerly inexhaustible variety of poetic themes, the mere enumeration and examination of them would hardly offer a satisfactory explanation of poetic thinking as such; nor would it yield a grasp of its essence and invariable substance crystallized in the typical configurations and structures of any poem whatsoever. It is precisely the form of poetic discourse and cognition, its general mode of construction, that distinguishes it in an obvious way from all other linguistic creations—which, culminating in concept-building and cognition (as does, for instance, science), issue in the domination of the world by the use of the lights gained thereby and by means of technology.

16

(Nothing of this kind is attempted in poetry.) The basic origin of poetic creation may also be distinct from that of other linguistic productions—that is, from the remaining structures of knowledge. And it is precisely the process of poetic thinking which we mean to describe and to analyze.

To anticipate: I shall attempt to show that the psychic organization of the poet is a phenomenon of mental regression and to demonstrate the kinship of this thinking type with that of the child and primitive man: and, indeed, this specific thought-activity will be presented and explained through an analysis of the *form* of poetic creations.

As object-study I shall for reasons of expediency choose in the first place the purest embodiment of poetic activity: namely, lyric poetry in its rhymed and rhythmic form.

Now, a certain sensuous plastic quality made up of optical and sound values characterizes the poetic product: 1) of *optical values,* insofar as it is governed by a comparison-symbolism (this may be a simple simile or its derivatives, symbol proper, metaphor, hyperbole, and so forth); 2) of *sound-values* by means of musical mastery of the word-stuff through rhythm and rhyme but also through sound- and word-painting in the broadest sense. Where does the source of such a kind of cognition lie?

The poet creates in an affective state. That clarity and sobriety which is the mark of other kinds of mental activity is lacking in his work. During realistic thinking, the emotions are muted, and their unconscious background is relatively quiescent. Far more intimate, however, is the connection of the world revealed by the poem with the poet's own range of feelings. During his creation the poet is in the throes of a special excitement which manifests itself even physically. The reason of this specific excitability may no doubt be traced back to a predisposition brought along by the poet, but, at the same time, only certain objects are endowed with the special power of inducing poetic excitement. They are no doubt interwoven in a particular way with the emotive make-up of the creator so that through the release of that excitability they are simultaneously exhibited and thereby overcome. As a result of this excitation, concepts and images are swayed in their linguistic shape by a rhythmic, musical wave. Rhythm is a product of poetic excitement, a child of emotion.

There are two kinds of rhythm. One is eruptive, orgiastic, and devoid of uniformity. It is that of the chorus of ancient tragedy, the dithyrambic rhythm, and the free rhythm loved by all romantics. One can rightly call it either dithyrambic or romantic. It stems from a poet's very violent affective excitement. The countenance of this rhythm, perhaps comparable to a fever curve if presented graphically, reflects the degree of the emotional excitement in the poet's mind. But since it nevertheless always remains a rhythm, and not a chaotic tumult, it still retains the formational element and therefore fulfills the most important function of rhythm: it controls the mental stuff of ideas as their linguistic container, their outer shape; it forms order out of chaos. And only such a rhythm in its very agitation is powerful enough completely to hold in thrall the ideas produced by such savage and fierce emotions. In a quieter stream all of the violent agitation could not be discharged to the outside. There would remain a painful and not yet objectivized residue. Only this kind of rhythm is able to incorporate satisfactorily those ideas welling out of the unconscious, to tackle them, so that, after they have become conscious, and then controlled, and mastered, the mind of the poet can free itself from them. Only thus do they become an object of the poet's act of appropriation in the form of cognition. Only this kind of rhythm is able to reflect the temper of the poetic soul, the frame of the poetic mind. Then flowing in its course, rhythm rocks the soul of the creator to sleep.

A second kind of rhythm is found in epic, dramatic, and also in lyrical poetry: it is that, for example, of the iamb of the drama, the Homeric hexameter, terza rima, eight-lined stanzas, sonnets, and so forth. One may call this the classic rhythm. Here the entwining, the constraining, sleep-inducing (soporific), and soothing function of rhythm becomes clearly apparent. During the creative process the mind of the poet is fixed on the inner world of his ideas and recites them in a chant.

This cleaving to an inner imaginary world, to a dreamlike content, is essential for the differentiation of poetical from scientific and, in general, from any practical activity of thinking. In the latter case *attention* is riveted on real or remembered (real) objects, not on configurations deviating from reality. This remains a fact even if an object seemingly belonging to "reality" is described in the poem. This "description" has an emotional source, and the whole mental effort of that "description" aims only at the psychic "overcoming" of the impression evoked by the described object. When the rows of ideas range themselves in the uniform channels of rhythm, the psyche of the poet, having mastered its agony musically and conquered it by musical harmony, is relieved of them.

The human mind seems to be equipped with a drive for "order." Rhythm seems to be an emanation of this ordering drive brought forth by the soul for the containment of tumultuously agitated ideas. The psyche obviously has the tendency as a means of self-preservation to get rid of all stimuli alien to it, to become cognizant of their causes, to gain clarity about them so as to dilute and (or) to eliminate them. It succeeds in this endeavor the sooner as it "orders" the stimulus-material. This is the task rhythm has to perform.

While order within the confines of scientific, realistic-analytical thought* embraces only the *material of ideas*

---

* I call scientific thinking realistic-analytic because it attempts to remain free of subjective elements and clings to the world of experience, and—as the history of natural sciences shows—strives for a reduction of the empirical objects to their elements, which then figure by way of mental construction as more general concepts.

as it arranges their elements according to their real similarity, entraps them in concepts and thus dominates them, that ordering through the poetic creative process engulfs also the *verbal material* in its topographical position. The ordering drive dominates the cognitive impulse of the psyche, it pushes to cognition and awareness (to knowing and becoming conscious) and is rooted in the will to appropriation and thus, simultaneously, in the will to self-liberation (through appropriation). Now in the psychic condition of poetic creation this drive for order is stimulated more vehemently; hence it affects the material substance of the words. The verbal material functions within the poetic thinking process not merely as a sign but also as matter, as a substitute of and for reality. The word here acquires the independent value of stuff or substance. World and word are gripped by a frenzy which wants to order, tame, and clarify; to conquer and possess the world and the one soul by means of words: that is, by dint of the specific qualities inherent in the words. The verbal material, the word-stuff itself, is supposed to depict world and soul simultaneously. This mental behavior is primitive, however, archaic and alien to scientific thinking. The primitive type of poetic thinking-activity thus in evidence is released by the higher degree of excitement of the poetic psyche, by poetic ecstasy. A symptom of the diminution of the reality-value of this thinking-activity is precisely the transference of the ordering factor to the word-mass, the sound-material.

Rhythm consists essentially of the *repetition* of equally

long or short, of accented or unaccented, syllables, of *equal* sound-values. In its bare outline the pattern of rhythm appears as repetition, as *regular* recurrence of equal sound-values. But the whole associative activity of a mind which is awake, the alpha and omega of the thought-process, is grounded in the connection of equal (or similar) contents of perception. This is therefore a mechanism founded on the principle of reiteration. But while the associative activity of conceptual thought aims primarily at the connection, the ordering (serial arrangement), of *visual* contents; rhythm manifests that search of the mind for equal elements, that craving of the soul again and again to create and to connect equal things, that spinning and weaving of the soul in the arranging of similar acoustic elements. Seen in this way, rhythm too is a mechanical association of equal *acoustical* units, whereas the (more) intellectual association by similarity is a conjunction of similar *visual* elements. Rhythm is obviously nothing other than the acoustic form of associational activity engendered by the stormy desire of the human mind for order, clarity, and the rest which alone can sustain the psyche in its autarchy against the world and, as a consequence, to assure its domination over it. The basis of this need is clear: it is knowledge whose very existence would become unmanageable indeed if the world and the contents of perception were to lie about in our minds like chaotic congeries of disparate and dissimilar (that is, diverse) particles. Such a chaos would wreck our minds. Only the existence of patterns of similarity, only the combinability of things makes possible the existence of consciousness in general, and beyond and above this, even the existence of life itself, the mastery of a world of objects. To connect like things and to segregate the unlike, to sunder and to distinguish, is all there is to the activity of the understanding. In human mentality, ordering, the drive to classify, is basic. Instructive of what the emergence of something absolutely strange and unfamiliar, hence of a content not assimilable into consciousness, may cause, is the fate of an African who was seized by madness at his first view of a large European steamship.

Rhythm arises because of the greater excitement of the poet's mind. The language of scientific discourse lacks emotional stress, and its words are not swept by feelings. The language of poetry, however, is affected by the force of emotions (anger, love, indignation) which change the structure of the sentences. It is possible to read off the mood of the poet from the tempo of his rhythm. Fatigue, reverie are put into and transcribed by a dragging rhythm, enthusiasm by a rushing one. Rhythm is the breath of the soul.

But just because the wording—the sound-stuff—is carried along by the stream of emotion, the reality-value of the description is reduced. A description of the world is intended, but rhythm catches up with the description and transforms it into music. The world cannot be described calmly and with clarity because the spirit of the creator is so violently shaken by the subject matter of the description that an additional task springs upon the mind of the poet unawares: how is it to present its own mental anguish, its emotional eruption? The poet now tries (indeed, he is compelled) to tackle the stirred-up, floating word-stuff. Collocated between these two tasks, the mind fails. Whatever the description gains in musical liveliness (in self-description), it is bound to lose in terms of other reality-values. For even if the tempo of this rhythm imitates not only the ups and downs of the feelings of the poet (the music of the poetic soul, but also the music of things) as they were sensed by the poet, such an accrual of purely musical acoustic values cannot compensate for the loss of reality-value that comes about through the transformation of the word-stuff into music. Thus we see that in poetry the word-stuff is entrusted with a double function: on one hand it is a conceptual symbol, on the other a musical element. Thus the word is granted autonomy and substance; it is raised into an end in itself because the description is a double one: as in every form of discourse, by way of the conceptual value of the word, but, over and above this, by way of the word-stuff itself, by the sound-matter—and even by its position and mechanical structure.

Rhythm is the means of abolishing the tense fixation on reality and the attention to reality which are the mark of prosaic thought-activity; of abolishing that tension which creates attention and forms the basic presupposition of realistic-analytic thought. Rhythm exercises that softly blunting effect which starts with the removal of attention. The elimination of tenseness, of the activity of consciousness, and the levelling of the direct, not musically veiled, relation to the outside world afford satisfaction to the human mind. This elimination is a return of the subject to itself, a retreat of the psyche, a detachment from the world, and a return homeward to an original passivity.

The human psyche, when it suffers and is gripped in a positive or negative way by the force of its ideas, needs the deadening effect of the narcotic of rhythm.

The phenomenon of rhythm affords the mind a double satisfaction: first, the flowing off of the emotional tension into the fixed paths of equalization through the rhythmical, the enfolding and the control of the agitated word-mass; second, the assuagement of emotions dampened and lulled to sleep by the monotony of sameness, by the recurrence of the alike, by the rocking of the rhythm. And it is the surprising characteristic of rhythm that it is born in agitation and is an ecstasy, but that it leads to sleep, to self-extinction. There are related phenomena, however. The intellectual functions of the mind are similarly destined to lead to a state of cloudless repose through cognition, i.e., through the grasp of an alien content that has penetrated into the mind and its dilution. And in reverting to repose, rhythm brings about self-annihilation and sleep. It is in *flowing* that excitement dissolves into rhythm; when it melts away and the energy of emotion is exhausted, sleep sets in.

The poetic excitement which is generated by the affec-

tive ingredients of the objects of description (that is, of
the subject matter) has the following result: the word
which was supposed to mirror the world is forced by
ecstasy to portray also the feeling-tempo of the poetic
psyche. In this way the word acquires, apart from its
conceptual function, the additional one of the expression
of feeling. The rhythmically ordered words must therefore render either the *subjective* rhythm, which is the
rhythm of feelings in the poet's soul brought about by
the stimulus-objects, the music of the soul accompanying
his ideas; or the *objective* rhythm—that is, the music of
things which the poet imputes to those objects themselves. Whether they are emanations of the mind of the
poet or symbolic objects evolved by him, they nevertheless possess their own musical worth, their immanent
feeling-value, as independent beings. (This is the case,
for instance, if the sadness or joy depicted is not the
poet's but someone else's and carries the rhythm proper
to that person; or if a thing of some kind is described
with the rhythm illustrative of it.) To be sure both kinds
of rhythm, the subjective as well as the objective, ultimately have a subjective origin, for what is always mir-
rored and communicated are the vibrations of feeling
which have arisen in the poet's soul on the margin of
things.

Thus the description becomes sensuous by means of
the rhythmic order. Alongside its formal symbolic significance as concept and sign, the word gains an autono-
mous material value; the definite rhythmic arrangement

of sound becomes the expression and a transcription of the feeling-tempo, of the state of the poet's affectivity. This description does not proceed, however, in the intellectual way through conceptual representation of facts (that is, indirectly), but directly by way of phonic portraiture—that is, by setting up a sound-structure whose stream corresponds materially to the inner stream of feeling, expresses it, replaces it, and is related to it as one member of an equation to the other one. Since the mood is not communicated intellectually through a train of concepts, this directness and immediacy of presentation is primitive: the emotions are overcome and dissolved mechanically as a verbal order is set up whose tempo matches the tempo of feeling. This mode of presentation is compulsive in origin; it is forced upon the creator by his state of mind. The emotional sweep engulfs the speech and rushes it along. The words materially portray the state of mind and impress on the presentation the mark of augmented sensuousness and materiality but, at the same time, also of primitivity. The discourse reverts to imitational gesticulation: it is a transcript, not a description.

We must bear in mind (and I shall deal with this later) that the word was originally not merely a sign, but also an expression of emotion, a cry; and that, being the expression and the imitation of the mood evoked in the mind of the speaker by the subject matter (that is, the referent of the concept), it already had an embryonic rhythmical value. Thus the word possessed a musical

27

value gradually lost through wear and tear (that is, through frequent use); and we may therefore consider the phenomenon of rhythm, of musical speech, as the restoration of the original expressive value of the word —namely, of its musical expressive value as the imitation of the tempo of the emotional agitation aroused by the object. Consequently, rhythm reawakens the archaic expressive function of the verbal utterance. We may envisage a poem or a single consummate sentence as a word-aggregate (as *one* word and *one* image) fluctuating musically to and fro according to the internal motions of affectivity.

Poetic language reproduces the vibrations of the affectivity which is tied to concepts; apart from its role as symbolical sign, the poetic word has the significance of a purely material expression of the feeling-tempo.

We hold this junction of emotional expression with conceptual symbolism as the revival of the original role of the word and of its sensuous value. If we regard the prosaic word with regard to emotion as a colorless point, then poetic excitement would bestow sensuous values on this neutral blank, this mere sign, or restore them to it: in one direction—the *acoustical* one—those sensuous values of musical expression—pure music could then be envisaged as an extension of this line; while in the opposite direction—the *visual* one—the values of plastic suggestivity would unfold in such a way that wordless visual art could be considered an extension of this aspect of verbal expression. We assume of course that both kinds of expressive value—the musical as well as the plastic—were inherent in the primitive word and have now been restored by the poet because of that ecstasy which carried him back into the original status of the sensuous, word-creative mode of thinking.

The rhythmic organization of a series of words, the order created by the poet, is a boon for the appreciator because in the structuring of the verbal material the clarity of the text is augmented and is made more manageable. The human mind becomes attuned to the regular recurrence of a definite syllabic pattern; the rhythmic flow is in itself a mnemonic prop: it enhances materially the sensuous quality of the whole train of ideas. Plasticity is increased; the vigor, the suggestiveness, and the palpability of the color of the presentation becomes stronger because the rhythmic emphasis stresses certain words pregnant with stronger affective content and accentuates them as for instance in,

Sing the *anger,* oh goddess, of the Pelid Achilles.

2

The Psychic Function of Rhythm and Rhyme

Like rhythm, rhyme is a binding agent, a means of mechanical association and ordering supposed to augment the effect of rhythm. The associative function which characterizes repetition becomes manifest also in rhyme. And rhyme too evokes that lulling narcotic effect of repetition, of uniformity, the sought-for dulling of consciousness. In rhythm, accented and unaccented, long and short, syllables recur in equal intervals; in rhyme syllable-color, similar sound, is repeated. Rhyme intensifies the ordering, and as a result, the calming effect of rhythm, its soporific action issuing from regular recurrence. It enhances the plasticity and impressiveness of appropriate word-pairs and becomes the suggestive vehicle for strengthening the material, sensuous values of expression hidden in the sound.

Rhythmicity, the musically basic form, remains constant, but rhyme as a poetical medium is by no means universal and is unknown to whole ethnic groups or periods of culture (antiquity, for example). Whether it occurs in the form of similar syllables at the ends of stanzas or as alliteration at their beginnings, or, as in the *Nibelungenlied,* as special accentuation within the stave, these nuances still oscillate within the range of the principle of repetition, of recurrence, of equal measure; the scheme remains that of controlling presentation through ordering. In the rhymed work the organizing element takes hold even of the sound-color, not merely of the "numbers" of sounds. The cradle of the soul becomes more all-embracing. The portrayal of the inner vibrations, of the soul-music accompanying the content of the ideas, becomes more adequate to its prototype. A photograph of the "mood" is to be achieved by ranging definite sound-values ordered as to accentuation and color. Equality of sound through rhyme strengthens and stiffens the rhythmic frame. But in addition the mechanicity and materiality of the musical mode of presentation is stressed by the superstructure of sound-similarity. Yet rhyme often has an element of sound-painting, of syllable-symbolism, of onomatopoeia, which I shall treat further below.

When the psyche of the poet falls into vibration, it tries with musical devices to squeeze its conceptual content into a state of order so that it can the more easily free itself from it; it tries to master those ideas by incorporating them and thus becoming more aware of them. As those means lead to the psychic control of those ideas, they facilitate the awareness of them. They thus free the mind and thereafter rock it to sleep—in fulfillment of the ulterior function of rhythm. To be sure, this organizing activity works with mechanical means. It affects only the verbal mass (that is, the mass of sound); it coordinates the verbal stuff and the color of syllables; on this plane it does not use the intellectually higher type of association by similarity which also has organizing power. This kind of order stems from the circulation of the blood and breathing, not from reason. It is the result of an overpowering affect, of intellectual devolution.

Within the framework of poetic thinking the word-stuff in order to fix the world is not in a state of rest; as a tremor grips the soul of the poet, the word-stuff responds to the swingings of affectivity, it sways more vehemently, and it expresses them. The syllables are set into motion and carry out that rhythmical dance which has something of the dance of savages. During the creative process the poet finds himself in the psychic situation of a primitive person who breaks out in words in order to release his affect, his mental affliction. The color of rhythm, bright and clear, its tempo, stormy or wary, depends on the mood of the poet's affectivity. It reflects his level of emotion. The words pulsate as do the feelings. If the poet narrates, cries out, or laments, slowly in grief, impetuously in rapture, an appropriate rhythm is ready for every situation. Iambs, dactyls, mixtures: every poem has its natural rhythm. The face of rhythm is an expression of the poet's face, the diagram of the movements of his affectivity.

As soon as the inner movement has carried away the verbal stuff, it streams forth, set in motion by rhythm. In order not to capsize, the flow of words looks for a measure, its own measure, a subduing measure. Thus rhythm in its impetuosity turns into a harmony whose physiological consequence is ease of mind. The sputtering current defeats itself. Because of its intensity, it achieves measure, its proper channeling and flow, the order which a strong stream will always dig for itself, but the emotions must not be overwhelming if it is to turn into poetic expression. If it is to be poetically controlled, it must be able to move into consciousness in form of images. If it overpowers the mind entirely, then neither image nor rhythm will follow, but silence or frenzy. This, then, is the debacle of the soul. It must not be entirely crushed; it must still retain some power of control in order to be able to speak.

In order to visualize the *effect of rhythm* let us imagine the regular knock of a small silver hammer against metal. Alongside the rousing effect, the recurrence of the regular beat by the silver mallet has also a soporific effect issuing from monotony. Poetic agitation as it turns into flow engenders rhythm. The accentuated syllables, the waking-points, represent the beat, the scratch, the instants of arousal; yet they all add up to a sleep-inducing pattern. The repetitive order of stanzas turns into the regular recurrence of equal musical-acoustical values and expands into an over-all soporific monotony. The order of the sound-stuff has a soothing effect because it results in a mastery—albeit a mechanical one—of the stimulus-material by the psyche, and allows it relief and alleviation.

When the poetic order has subdued the emotional disturbance, consciousness gains the upper hand, but in the ensuing phase it fades away; it lulls itself to sleep. The monotony of the verse-order physiologically evokes a sleep-like state. Now the sleep-wish, the desire for the elimination of the animation of consciousness, of psychical tension, is a basic wish of human beings. Half of life —that of sleep—succumbs to it, while the other—the waking half—is consumed by longing for it.

The invasion of a chaos of new sensations and impressions, all impinging on the world of feelings without being assimilated by it, is agonizing for the psyche. They disturb its equilibrium, the quiescence of its emotions. Thus they disturb the relative sleep. This onslaught of the eternally novel and undigested constitutes the agony of the psyche which can free itself only in resolving the novel, the disturbing, and the jamming, and in incorporating it; in adjusting it to the existing system of ideas, and harmonizing it with the order of feelings—that is, in mastering it intellectually and in getting over it emotionally. The assimilation must be a double one: integration within the world of feelings through expression and within the realistic-analytic system of thought through cognition. In its rudimentary stage poetry in prehistoric times satisfied these two needs; now, however, it implements the first task in attaching itself to ideas which are not yet ripe for assimilation by the realistic system of thought or which are permanently unassimilable by it owing to their content and their emotional saturation. These new ideas or feelings appear first on the retina of consciousness, then dip down, mostly uncomprehended —as foreign bodies, disturbing and unconquered—into the recesses of the psyche to cause a malaise that can only be overcome when those disturbances are dissolved in a regular process of ascent into consciousness—that is, can be worked off by both expression and cognition.

The psychic tension, the dilation caused by an unassimilated train of ideas, is a transient stage which is being resolved by expression and reason (this is what "becoming fully conscious" means) and then cedes to peace of mind; then the soul as it were enters into a passive, satisfactory, sleep-like, horizontal position. When the emotional congestion unloosens, when the attitude of watchfulness and attention to the surrounding world—to the ideas requiring mental incorporation—is untied, when the disturbance has been removed because it has been expressed, lifted, and worked off in an internal effort, a state of waking passivity ensues. This halcyon calm is not consciousness any more, but its twilight, a waking sleep hovering on the borders of real sleep.

The soul is as it were an organ coveting metaconsciousness through consciousness, and it is able to reach it if the whole process succeeds. The mainspring of all thinking is the wish for its elimination and the reversion to a state of peace, to the intellectual position of a childlike brain. It may be true that the psyche out of a kind of interest in self-preservation is driving toward the elimination of the disturbing material, but it is precisely this, a *desire for an inner blank,* an *urge for sleep,* for *unconsciousness,* a will to a *homeward return to a dormant ego,* which basically is certainly identical with the *longing for death,* for an anorganic existence, for **nonbeing,** except that this yearning for death is coupled—in conscious moments—with the fear of death as something unknown, unconceived, and inconceivable. The impulse for self-preservation and the death-wish coincide in the primeval drive for quiescence and inertia.

Thus rhythm as an associative concatenation of the verbal material may be conceived as the reenactment of the acoustical-musical values of presentation and expression inherent in the primeval word. It appears as the instrument of expression and presentation which the psyche creates for itself because it must do so in a certain constellation of agitation in order adequately to reflect itself, to facilitate the removal of the aggravating stimulus-materials, to master the annoying contents through an act of consciousness, to work them off through expression, and thus to enter into the peace of unconsciousness. It is precisely the element of subdual through order (arrangement) and repetition that serves this purpose: incorporation of the contents and creation of a sleeplike psychic state through monotony (uniformity). The emotion is worked off when the affective state of soul is portrayed by rhythm. It finds its adequate expression in rhythm because here something objective (extrinsic) is set up which equates (and thus replaces) the subjective (intrinsic) state.

Up to now the events in the mind of the poet, of the maker, have been described. As for the processes in the psyche of the appreciator and therefore of psychology of art-enjoyment, the following may be anticipated: we have seen thus far that to the waking state per se, to the exertion of will, to the effort of attention, there inheres something painful and that the psyche strives for inner repose, a smoothing down. But if an impression of a sensation is to take place, the surface-mirror of the mind must be titillated by a minimum of novel sensations. It must be a certain "plus"—which does not go so far as to churn and then to dive down, uncomprehended and unsolvable, into the recesses of the soul, but something that may be understood and assimilated at once. If pleasure is to occur, then a soft wavy motion must affect the mirror of the soul, a stimulant, as it were a feeble reveille, some variation. Now this constitutes the magic of the poetic diction, the pleasurable aspect of poetic dream-thinking, that it leaves a consciousness lulled to sleep, subdued but more colorful. It is a dream-state not possessing the tension of attentiveness, yet immersed in song, which could be described as painless and still "stimulating" awareness which being moderate in its mode, would be most likely to suit the need of life (for stimulation) and that of death (or rather sleep). This may explain the peculiar state of thrill and excitement which enraptures the enjoyer of poetic creation. He finds himself in a state which is a mixture of sleep and awareness, a world constructed out of rhythm, word and image, suggestion and concept, an enjoyment of images, not of clear analytical thinking which requires an unceasing exertion of will, consequently of struggle or its variant: work; and at the same time it pales into colorlessness so as to become scarcely visual. Here we have a lower species of consciousness, composed of somnific, stimulative, imagistic and thought-elements, a sensuous and dreamlike thinking in which visual and acoustical experience predominates.

The state of mind into which the enjoyer is transported is a repetition in duller colors of the poetic experience, a reliving of the psychic process in which the poet found himself during the process of creation. As the mind of the poet was freed through adequate expression, his inner self relieved through its externalized representation, so now the enjoyer follows in the footsteps of the poet on his way of pain and deliverance.

3

The Symbol-Structure of Poetic Thinking

If we now turn to the conceptual aspect, to the inner form of poetic thinking, we see that the most important characteristic of poetic discourse is its symbolism. The specific plasticity of poetic language is grounded in it. This symbolic thinking can manifest itself grammatically in various ways: as simile, metaphor, allegory, or genuine symbol. *All of these forms are rooted in comparison.* For instance, the symbol is a truncated comparison, one member of which, the *prima comparationis,* is left out through a process of condensation.

The source of this symbolic thinking is to be found in poetic ecstasy. It has leveled one intellectual stratum, the one fitted for realistic and thus the scientific thinking which was acquired by human beings latest in their development. Scientific thinking is marked by a clear relationship to reality, by an attention to and an unceasing alertness toward objects. It also has the critical power of discernment, a subjective disinterestedness, which renders possible the definite cleavage of the world into subject and object and the discrimination of the objects among themselves. It, finally, has the sobriety that enables us to examine reality, to search and analyze, to split things and to decompose them into homologous elements which then serve as concepts of a higher order.

The powerful excitement of the poetic mind has eliminated those subtler intellectual capacities for thought, so that the mind is solely able to grasp that which falls primarily within the range of the senses, within the sensuous, the visual, as it were, the perceptual patches, the color spots which emerge like a wreckage out of the tempestuous ocean. The elements which captivate the interests of the psyche in this state are mostly those which have been for a long time ingrained through habit and experience in its deeper strata and are therefore instinct with an inveterate affective relationship to it. These are ideas which slumber for a long time as remembrances within the depths of the soul and therefore are predestined to become symbols of its most potent interests (whether these concern feelings or objects of the external world). When the mind is churned, those images rise to the surface as though spontaneously. Since it is intent on freeing itself from its painful contents pressing upwards to the surface from its depths, the soul seizes upon them in its thirst for self-consciousness. The agitation is too strong to permit quiet examination, self-analysis and object-analysis; therefore the mind, as a means of interpreting the objects of distress, empties the receptacle of its ideas and hauls up the tools of comparison (*secunda comparationis*) which drift to the surface —so that in becoming clearly conscious of them it can shake them off. In its feverish condition the intellect is capable of achieving only this.

But this associational method is different from the usual one. If the poet is trying to free himself from the contents of a compelling idea says: *deine Augen sind so schoen wie die Sterne* (your eyes are as beautiful as the stars), he is not following the example of a logician, who says "A lion is an animal"; he is making associations not according to factual similarity of the two objects, but according to a sensuous aspect which has obtruded on his feeling—that is, according to the impression the compared object calls forth in his mind. The *impressions* which the eyes and stars make upon him are akin. In this particular case the impression has been called forth because of a love for certain eyes. Thus the poet compares two *impressions,* and not two *objects.* He associates those objects according to the similarity of the *impression* established in his mind by them, according to the similarity of the *affect* (*emotion*) generated by them. The poetic comparison (i.e., the simile) is subjectively conditioned, the judgment subjectively distorted. The distortion ensues for the benefit of the emotionally stressed *prima comparationis;* in the case at hand, it is transfigured by love, namely, by that for the eyes. By means of this simile the poet wants to describe not only the kind of bliss, but also the strength of the impression which the loved object created in him. He can disengage himself from the excessive bliss which the beloved eyes bestowed on him, and "explain it away" only by drawing attention to his being reminded of the beneficent effect and the power of its radiance. No astronomer, not even an ignorant peasant, will discern similarity to fact here; only a feverish intellect alienated from reality chances upon this analogy, emotionally determined and rooted as it is in the love-affect. A certain exaggeration too is always characteristic of poetic discourse whenever it uses a simile or any other poetic figure at all—an exuberance that recalls the enthusiasm with which the lover meets the loved object. Poetic agitation seems to be akin to erotic excitement. Love and hate, compassion and contempt—the poet lays these into the objects he describes; feelings bring forth the word and the enchanted images, the exaggerations of an enamored mind. For his emotion-laden intellect is capable only of this kind of imagistic thinking.

As a result of the foregoing analysis of the poetic simile, the nature of poetic ecstasy has become clearer. It cannot be asserted that there exists a specifically poetic ecstasy alien to all other non-poetic minds. Feelings that are common to all men engender in the psyche of the poet the need of representation which is satisfied in the poetic manner. All the world feels love or hate, and everybody has in his mind objects affected by such emotions—as it were ideas dwelling in the penumbra of emotion and slumbering on the floor of the psyche. It may be that a non-poet possesses fewer ideas of this kind, and that to poets more objects attain an affective meaning. The poet's relationship to the outer world may be closer perhaps because of a more richly developed inner life.

Either such ideas do not evoke in the non-poet a need for representation—perhaps because the feelings that could release it are less intense—or perhaps this compensatory representational need is present in everybody but fails to become satisfied because of an intellectual insufficiency. It is precisely the poet who must lend speech to the dumb. Not just everybody has the capacity for poetic association. No simile may occur to him, since after all this occurrence too is an intellectual achievement *sui generis,* even if engendered by emotion; it is an ability which carries with it the creative capacity for seeing and combining.

In the well-known poem—

> *Ein Fichtenbaum steht einsam*
> *Im Norden auf kahler Höh'.*
> *Ihn schläfert; mit weisser Decke*
> *Umhüllen ihn Eis und Schnee.*
> *Er träumt von einer Palme,*
> *Die fern im Morgenland*
> *Einsam und schweigsam trauert*
> *Auf brennender Felsenwand.*

> (A spruce-tree stands alone
> in the North on naked heights.
> It sleeps; with a white covering
> ice and snow envelope it.
> It dreams about a palm-tree
> which far away in the Orient
> grieves lonely and silent
> on a wall of burning rocks.)

—the poet compares himself with a spruce in the North, his beloved with a palm-tree in the South so as to intimate by these symbols first, the physical looks of the persons mentioned, but second and foremost, to show the power of longing and its unrealizability because of distance. The distance is also to be interpreted symbolically, however, because what is hinted at is not the physical, but the psychical distance. In this simile it is obviously not any real similarity that matters to the poet, but the impression that the unattainable beloved evoked in the poet's heart comparable for him to the impression that the dreamed of but distant palm-tree must evoke in him, the man in the North. Accordingly this is a subjective kind of association through and through, one that is kept within the compass of similarity of personal impressions (not of things). As against this, an association according to real similarity in realistic analytical thought arranges the things into classes. This leads to concept-building so that higher types of concepts correspond to new classes; this results in genuine cognition of the world and hence to the *intellectual mastery of its objects*. The poet achieves nothing of this sort; he achieves solely a *liberation* from the painful burden of a mood, a feeling, through visionary (symbol-laden), emotionally saturated description in musical, rhythmical dress. This constitutes a special kind of awareness (*Bewusstwerden*) whose psychical aim differs from that of realistic, scientific description and explanation.

But what subjects do become so oppressive in a poetical sense (that is, do distress the poet)? What must be their nature if they are to release poetic reaction? The following example can make the question explicit:

My friend was writing in his library on a typewriter that had just been delivered. His six-year-old daughter Hansi, who was not acquainted with this contraption, out of curiosity came repeatedly into the library to fathom the mystery of the writing-machine. Constantly she tried to busy herself with the mechanism and thus disturbed her father in his work. As repeated admonitions bore no fruit, the father finally yelled in disgust at the disobedient Hansi and sent her from the room. Hansi was very grieved about this, took a piece of cardboard and with a few strokes drew on it a table as a surface on which the machine was standing outlined by dots. In front of it was the approximate contour of a grown human figure sitting on a chair, and on the other end of the table a puny figure on a footstool. On the upper part of the drawing she wrote with block letters: PAPA SHOUTS AT HANSI. Here we see the classical example of a psychic situation out of which the artistic reaction is bound to result. It does so in the first place when—because of the facts of the case—the individual is prevented from responding by means of action to counter his affliction. In other words the situation is one of psychic helplessness in which the artistic reaction is the appropriate remedial counter-measure and the only one available.

The artistic subject matter must therefore be of such a kind on the poet's side as to exclude any other form of clearance except the poetical one. Any other reaction would be impossible and ineffective and would not result in a psychic relief for the poet. Any other sort of clearance is impossible too because the feelings of the poet are shaken to such depths by the affect-charged stimulus that all he is able to desire at this juncture is the expression of this feeling. He is forced above all to describe this state of his feelings: love, pain, distress. If he limits himself to describe only the subjective feeling, he is a lyrical poet, but if he proceeds to describe also the cause of his feelings, he creates epics or a drama. If the poet wants to express what social involvement, what adverse fate, torments him, then he must represent this fate and the feeling resulting from it in order to lift the distressing complex into consciousness and thus to attain clearance from it. The peremptory expressive need craves for the poetic forms as the only adequate and satisfactory means of relief. In the poem quoted above the poet had recourse to a palm-tree to illustrate his longing by an object which, as a fountain-head of feeling, resembled his beloved. He did so on compulsion since only the far-off palm-tree was apt to express properly his love and his longing. In his emotional upheaval the poet is incapable of scientific analysis and equally powerless for action. He therefore attempts neither to examine nor to explain, but to express.* And if he achieves *expression,* his mind is lighter of one burden. But he *must* resort to expression because nothing else could relieve him. It may well be that in an analogous psychical situation everybody, provided that the poet's means were available to him, would resort to the poetic technique in order to assuage the expressive need. As for the poet himself, it may be that the greater intensity of his feelings may require poetic clearance and that his superior associational ability may render it feasible.

In its primitive childlike stage human thinking knows no other method of association than that of making the simile (comparison)—that is, than the poetical one; originally "explanation" works solely with similes (comparisons): through adhibition of symbol-objects; thus primitive mythologies are nothing else than a system of similes. Because of its subjective character this association by means of simile differs profoundly from the logical association through similarity. Closer inspection would disclose that association by simile is rather a kind of

---

* In a similar psychic plight are those bewailing a beloved dead. A dirge is the only remedy left to them.

47

association through contiguity because the "similarity" of the two objects (members) of the simile, as a "similarity" mediated in the mind of its creator, is by reason of the "similarity" of the emotive impression of the two objects, entirely contingent. At bottom any conceivable object may be adduced by way of a simile for the benefit of an "explanation" of another one. The emotion-saturated individual easily discovers affinities everywhere because in his distress he is groping for symbol-objects for the sake of expression. In such a situation every object may potentially assume for the mind the explanatory power of a simile (symbol-object). Then the whole world lies before it as an array of symbol-bodies ready to serve as interpretations of feelings, to answer questions: briefly, a world full of affinities opens up. According to the "wealth of the imagination" of the creator, all the objects predestined to function as similes (and this is the whole world) lie side by side in an aura of emotion.

Ideas—such, for example, as love—generate a strong affect in the heart of the poet. His psyche wrestles with them until the poetic reaction sets in—that is, until the accessory affects are as it were transformed into motor energy and the distressing feelings are discharged outwards (expressed and represented). The excitement in the flash of poetic creativity is of course no longer an impulse of love or hate, but it is out of them—out of their accumulated affective energy—that the new psychic movement issues; thus, since a person who hates speaks differently from one who loves, even its very coloring depends on the character of the basic emotion. But this is no longer the emotion itself, which in a rather downright fashion has been converted into motor energy and now, in the form moulded by the specific poetic excitement, ejects its ideas out of the mind of the poet into the outer world. When the driving power of the discharged affective energy bursts forth, then the specific poetic excitement characteristic of the creative moment takes place.

As soon as the affectivity has in store a sufficient number of dischargeable ideas, production follows—that is, they are projected to the outside. Objects functioning as similes are adduced, and the wealth of the poet's mind begets an entire system of images. For a primitive person, perhaps one word or one outcry would have sufficed to effect an emotional discharge; but this is not always true of the mind of a modern poet filled with remembrances of ideas, images, and so forth. He does not say merely: "I love you" or "Oh, you beautiful fountain." His mind is relieved only after the emotion is discharged in an entire system of images and words.

The technique of poetic comparison (simile, symbol, metaphor, allegory, and so forth) constitutes a subjectively determined, archaic kind of association, the origin of which is the affect (emotion). Only feeling perceives similarities in the objects of the simile, which is the warp and woof of this associational method, which is therefore inferior in genuine reality-value to the intellectual association by (factual) similarity. If we inquire about the

49

ideas and feelings which require this symbolic treatment, we see that the undetermined, obscure ones and those of which one is not clearly aware are of moment. The affect has stirred up the psyche and suggested dim, uncertain ideas to it; and the poet searches in the external worlds for objects which might serve as incarnations, illustrations, and explanations of those ideas. He looks for things and relationships in the world of objects that seem to equate the contents of his mind in such a way that he can attain clarity about his inner self (the internal events through the interpretation of them by a second (external) series of things—which are interpretative of the first (internal) one and, as it were, topping it. The explanation of the inner state of affairs consists essentially of its recapitulation. Repetition is a clarifying procedure because what is repeated seems less strange.* The symbol-objects are in precisely those of the objects of the external world which are supposed to be akin to the psychic phenomena in need of explanation so that the latter may become embodied in the former. The psychic phenomena in need of externalization (that is, of description) seek support in the corporeality of the symbol-objects. Only when those psychic facts attain the solid foundation of the symbol (that is, when the object of the simile, the *secunda comparationis,* has been found), do they acquire any determined content (or reference) or meaning. The poet does indeed want to express something,

---

* And externalization is in itself an "explanation," "clarification."

but not merely the "how"; the "what" too is recondite, unclear to him. In the spiritual condition in which he finds himself as a result of his emotional perturbation, the poet expects deliverance from the symbol-objects which have offered themselves to him. He takes hold of them, but in so doing he determines not only the "how" (the form), but also the content of his presentation. The "idea" buried in the soul of the poet is too vague to be explained by anything other than a symbol, the object of a simile. It is too multifarious, too ambiguous, and too indefinite. It has neither name nor definition in the vocabulary of a language. It is only in the symbol-object that this idea becomes crystallized. It is in the invention of symbols that the activity of the poet is linguistically creative and verbally productive: namely, as invention of new designations for as yet unnamed and, consequently, unknown psychical aspects. Invention of symbols also constitutes linguistic invention and concept-formation, identical with and corresponding to the verbal invention of the just as speechless primitive man likewise struggling for expression.

The poet who was the first to call the earth "mother of men" possessed an obscure notion of the role of the earth as he created this metaphor. He wanted to express that the earth nourishes and takes care of human beings and that its attitude toward them is a mother's toward her child, and so forth. By using the word "mother" he as in a flash of lightning illustrated the position of the earth, and the store of meaning inherent in motherliness was transferred at one stroke to the earth. The love of the earth and for life, an obscure feeling, awoke an entire system of indefinite ideas which found corporeal consistency when the words, "Thou, earth, art a mother" were uttered. To explain the position of the earth, a being familiar in family life is turned into a symbol.

The analysis of a metaphor, "the blood of grapes" (signifying "wine"), reveals that it is supposed to express the power and the sweetness of wine, its qualities, its excellence, its value, but also its place in the body of the grape. The examination of the symbolism of the two preceding metaphors evinces the *anthropomorphic* spirit of the first and the downright *animistic* spirit of the second one; this primitivity is characteristic of the archaic regression of the poetic mind. We become aware that in its symbols the world of the conceptions of the poetic mind reduplicates the spirit of ancient cosmogonies.

The expression "blood-leech" applied to an evil man could be similarly analyzed as an example of a pejorative metaphor.

All objects can be used as symbol-objects (metaphorically, and so forth); but it is always some emotive attitude that points to some symbol-objects in which the symbolic affinity is discovered. The number of symbol-objects determines the wealth of the poet's intellect, of his so-called "imagination." Yet objects and relations of nature and of family life are used with predilection for symbolic ends. They are within easy reach of the creator and deeply embedded in his affective life, especially because they are often objects familiar to him from the experiences and remembrances of his childhood. It is mainly realistic objects that are supposed to interpret novel, recently developed, complex psychic structures.

The search for symbols in an act born out of the psychic struggle for clarity; it eventuates with organic necessity. It is compulsive by nature. The "plastic" form of the presentation and the poetic verbal artistry are not the intention. They are not purposeful; the poet follows no "esthetic" design; rather, there is a compelling need grown out of inner insufficiency, out of psychic want. Symbolism becomes affectation and ornateness at the hand of an imitator who lacks originality, or of a mere virtuoso who, having wrenched with cunning from out of his own nature the secret of the technique of the simile originating in the unconscious, now practices it professionally as a handicraft and transforms it into a skill. The virtuoso of symbolism who is acquainted with the effect of the symbolic style on human sensibility and therefore wants to re-evoke it, acts exactly as does the scientist who avails himself (technically) of the stores of power inherent in electricity through the repeated use of proper devices. There is a difference in the ethical estimation of their procedures, however, since the action of the scientific technician is morally indifferent or even meritorious, while that of the poetic virtuoso is reprehensible and should be condemned.

4

The Demarcation of Poetry and Science

When the psyche feels itself gripped from the outside, it can follow different courses; it can respond 1) by action, 2) through scientific exegesis, 3) through artistic creation (literature, sculpture, music). What the psyche selects as its self-saving expedient depends on the nature of the stimulus (of the affecting object) and on the character of the affected subject; but it also depends on the subject's own psychical attitude (the mental situation) at the moment. True, response will be different according to the nature of the person; for no two individuals ever react in the same way to one and the same stimulus. But there are certain typical reactions. If the psyche is intent upon the possession of a material object, it will respond with actions. A hungry person will usually not investigate the chemical characteristics of food-stuffs; but he

54

will grab and eat. On the other hand, someone who aspires to the rank of minister or ambassador, for instance, will not write a lyrical poem to achieve his purpose; he will perhaps arrange a mass meeting. In all of these cases the psyche is characterized by some *striving,* by a clear *objective,* which it reaches through a struggle with the outer world. The mental attitude is neither questioning or searching, as it is in scientific investigation; nor is it a struggle with an opaque content of consciousness for the purpose of expression and self-interpretation, as it is in art.

But a human being who grieves at the death of someone he loves or who is touched by the beauty of a wood will attempt to give verbal expression to his feelings; and, if he is a "poet" (that is, if he has association-making ability and also the impressionability of an artistic individual), will have recourse to poetic technique. It is true, of course, that not everyone who mourns the death of someone near to him grieves out loud; nor does he compose either a drama or a sonnet; but numbs himself with activity. These activities are only substitutes, however, not the natural reaction: In the realm of nature, grief follows pain, and any other behavior is a matter of training or education. The natural reaction is a mental struggle with an event saturated with emotion. The normal person complains verbally about the evil in order to "cope" with it; but, not having the poet's treasury of images at its disposal, his mind stands mute. He may also in individual cases be less sensitive than the poet.

If the artistic reaction is to result, the psyche must have suffered a hurt which will be healed through expression, through projection to the outside, through presentation, and through its being made conscious. The psyche behaves analogously with a wounded organism, which as a rule will not take recourse to a substitute to achieve numbness, but will tend its wound. Perhaps in the poetic mind sensibility outweighs motor forces; perhaps there is in it a certain disposition toward passivity. But the scientist too is marked by a passive posture, except that in him, as compared with the poet, the psychic attitude is different: namely, the type of thought is realistic, and the purpose of the thought-activity is different. For somebody searching for the source of artistic reaction, it is enlightening that a person who has undergone a painful experience also adopts a passive attitude similar to the artist's. His energy is as if paralyzed, and he indulges in observations about the reasons of his misfortune and the particulars of his present unhappiness. A woman too is inclined to react passively to external events.

Basically the scientific reaction is no less a controlling act of domination than is the artistic one. It is an act of force which achieves control by intellectual (mental) means: In the artistic sphere it succeeds through "expression." Painful ideas are conquered as they are made conscious and "expressed." In the scientific sphere they are conquered through investigation of the disquieting factors.

For the artist not every affect, along with the aura of

ideas (images) surrounding it, is due to become the occasion for poetic reaction. The death of a loved person will always call up violent affects, but they do not always press for artistic presentation. Only certain affective contents induce the special characteristic of poetic reaction: namely, only those for which the associations are stored which become activated as the poet searches for symbols. And even in the course of one and the same (artistic) life there will be periods when the creator responds differently, and sometimes not at all. A young man's reactions are quite different from those of an old man. Still, a summary view of artistic achievements of all times shows that the erotic sphere has always been the object of artistic reaction and has remained so. Originally this was not exclusively so at all. Originally, art and religion coincided, but they coincided also with the realm of thought which today is called science. Undifferentiated, these three intellectual realms lay together as a unit and then branched out in separate intellectual provinces; yet they have continued to influence each other, and the religious root of art especially cannot be eradicated and is clearly evident in the great artistic epochs.

It may be that those affective images which seize the mind of the poet in periods most important for the development of personality (childhood, for instance, and the period of puberty) are designated above all others to become objects of later artistic reaction. The power of artistic creativity (that is, of artistic form) may be derived only from those emotive ideas that have affected the artist in that period of life which was decisive for his personality development.

We should therefore delimit the art and sciences in terms of their different geneses. When the excitement of the psyche is of such an extent that a dull or stifling opaqueness of painful ideas results, the elimination of the disturbance by way of scientific reaction (clarification) would not constitute a liberation of mind: the mind in this state of agitation requires another remedy. Under these circumstances such an elimination through science would not even be possible. What is oppressive must be expressed, the opaque and dark must be brought into the open, and the affective ingredients must be motorally transferred into musical form. Only when the psychic contents are discharged in this way, will the mind be liberated. The motivational groundwork of these two "cognitive structures" (art and science) is different qualitatively, and the mental perturbation is differently constituted respectively. The scientific reaction is caused by an object of the outer (or inner) world in which is contained an element unknown to the investigator, an X, which the researcher is intent upon solving through analysis and through tracing it back to something which is known. For example, symptoms of illness are recognized, but the virus that provokes them is hidden. The multiplicity of animal species is known, but their origin is the object of investigation. Earthquakes are noted, but what causes them is enigmatical. As soon as that X, the source of the threat, is revealed (that is, when "the problem is set"), consciousness enters into a state of disinterested attention in order to explore reality. The attitude is that of the hunter stalking a deer. Here concern is always for a system of phenomena or events which do not directly threaten the scientific individual as such—that is, they do not threaten him "personally." They are therefore not of such vital immediate significance to the mind of the explorer or so pregnant with deep emotions as is, for instance, one's own experience of death or love. The origin of the mental uneasiness is a certain unknown existing externally.

The Poetic Species

By contrast, the object of the artistic reaction is never an object of the outer world as such (as in science), but always the affectively obscured idea, the emotionally embedded image of this object which calls forth the reaction because of its affective linkage with instincts, drives, and interests—the ideals of the creator. This idea calls for expression. "Reasons" are not pursued. But the object, because of the mental interest which it arouses, dips down into the psyche as an image colored in some special way, as a mysterious form and cause of inner unrest; being itself undetermined as to its content, it requires clarification. Then the psyche, wounded inwardly, must above all else bring about the crystallization of the contents of this image; must lay bare the content of the injury, and become aware of what happened, and how it did. The psyche must be able to say, "I love," or "I hate," or "I suffer." This self-clarification can come about in two ways: The images (the objects) and the stimuli themselves are being presented. The objects of emotion (of love or hate) are then projected from its affective angle, and thus the inward liberation from the feeling-complexes attached to them is reached. If this projection is carried out in the way mentioned, then one speaks of the "objective" literary art (epic, drama), although the whole procedure challenges any comparison as to its subjectivity. It is subjective through and through. For if the content of such a poetic vision and its relation to the creator are examined, one arrives at the conclusion that the projected forms for the most part symbolize the creator himself or some element of his being. Often these are actual experiences which he is trying to get rid of by means of presentation and projection; sometimes the projected characters embody urges and desires which hold opaque sway within the poet and press outward; thus, through the symbolic projection of the drive as figure or personage, the drive rises to consciousness and is conquered. The poet can of course also present personages of the outside world who arouse in him a passionate interest: these, however, are in fact only an extension of his poetic ego; they are beings whom the poet marks out with an impetuous acceptance or rejection. If they evoke his poetic hate, then they do indeed contain a psychic part of his ego; they then personify hated and inwardly resisted inclinations of his moral personality, leanings which he defeats by embodying them in fictional human figures. But there can also be figures of the outside world which engage his mind so deeply and which arouse his violent rejection so strongly that he must execute them symbolically (through presentation) as a just avenger, so to speak, in order to achieve and retain a tolerable relationship to the existing world-order. The first variety will occur more frequently, so that these characters reveal personified and projected natural tendencies of the poetic psyche; from this one can explain the passionate quality of the condemnation and the moral indignation. This pattern thus presents instances of the mental defense of the poet; the characters themselves are projected personifications of his struggle with his own evil and condemned propensities which are overcome when they are lifted out of their darkness and transferred as symbols to the outside.

The classification of poetry into objective and subjective can therefore *not* stand if confronted by psychological investigation. "Objectivity" is always something deceptive. But this much is right: that in epic and drama the complexes of feeling and interest find their embodiment in human figures; whereas the lyric tends to seem merely an endless variation of the sentence, "I feel," and not only an "I-content," but also an "I-form" prevails. Sometimes it is merely implied. The lyric posture has the peculiarity neither of presenting the object of the "disturbance" nor of introducing a drive in personified or active form, but of, so to speak, nakedly expressing the feeling caused by the "disturbance." The mind of the lyric poet is the more impressionable. He does not pursue the round-about path of personification (for it *is* a round-about path); the high degree of his emotion does not allow his feelings to swarm out as objective figures in an extended line. But the lyrical posture is historically the more primitive. And it is even today for the most part the preserve of the younger poet, representing as it does the original form of the poetic art with all its musical and sound-material qualities; thus it reflects the earliest form of the struggle with the obscure forces of the mind and reveals simultaneously the highest power of poetic emotion. It is emotion, then, which characterizes the earliest form of poetry but, at the same time also, there is closely related to it a relative poverty of the elements of experience, that is, a lack of the visual and visionary, as compared with the purely musical-elements. The former come into full blossom only in drama and epic. All of these particularities of lyrical poetry result quite naturally from the fact that epic-dramatic poetry presents the artist's affective ideas themselves as they personify his impulses and feelings and eject them out of his mind as objective figures; while lyrical poetry expresses merely the feelings attaching to those affective images or ideas.

The Archaic Structure of Poetic Thinking

By its very nature the psychic function of art differs from that of scientific research. And in each of these two mental stances a specific means of gratification is required for the psychic needs of the creator. The excitement of the mentally aroused artist flows off in symbols and music. In this sense form is the only adequate means by which the artist is liberated from the contest of excitation. The stimulus-object of the thinker is not an individual phenomenon as such, but as a type or class of a group of phenomena. By contrast it is a concrete individual case which interests the artist; it is a specific person, a certain relationship, a definite wood, a certain tree, or even the whole world conceived as an individual, as a personality. The mode of artistic presentation nevertheless acquires a typical value because on the one hand the artist himself constitutes a type, and therefore his mode of reaction becomes a typical one; and on the other hand the ground of the excitement is also a typical one since the stimulus, like any person and event, is not something singular or unique by nature. There would be no possibility of a mental effect on the person enjoying art if art were not to represent things which could awaken a response in him and which, because they are suitable for his mentality, could also arouse him; and if situations and emotions were not symbolized which are psychically accessible to him. For the possibility of artistic effect depends ultimately on a mental identity between the creator and the appreciator. The mind of the poet is not focussed on causes. He is not causality-minded and does not ask for causes. If he is moved by an object, he wants to become clear about his feelings. Mentally his position is not questioning and investigative, as is true of the researcher; but it is positive like that of a religious believer who struggles for the right expression of this obscure knowing. The thinker wants to *unveil* the world, the artist to *express* his ego. The mind of the former is directed toward the object, of the latter toward the subject (his own self). The poet overcomes the congestion in his mind by unloading it through word-creation, the word-material reproducing and replacing the object of emotion.

Symbolism is inspired by feelings. The symbol of palms and fir-trees, in the poem by Heine cited above, was prompted by yearning and unhappy love, and the fir-component also included self-compassion and self-love. The symbols must be "striking" in order to be entered into spiritually and emotively. But that appropriateness lies rather in the "how" of the saying than in what is said. For the invention of symbols is a discovery of analogies which can actually be found between any objects whatsoever, provided they are contemplated or looked at from a certain angle of vision.

It has already been pointed out that originally the entire realm of human knowledge was of a poetic nature —that is, was symbolic. The first thinkers were poets. The primitive cosmogonies were systems of "similes." Heavenly bodies and objects of nature were animized and endowed with human characteristics, the relationships of creatures in nature being approximated to those of the family, of house and yard, and generally of human surroundings. A human being would lend his passions to the things found in nature; and he conceived all *events* as *actions,* and all actions as human. All knowledge, indeed all the linguistic heritage, was nothing other than a system of similes. Men imputed the human psyche to nature and human action to the course of events, and compared the sphere of nature with the human sphere. As nothing outside the human sphere was known or conceivable, the extra-human was invested with a human quiddity and something familiar was brought into play for the explanation of something unfamiliar. But the word *itself* was also only a simile. It was compared with the object of its denotation so that it could replace this object materially. The word was thus the sonorous simile of the thing it denoted.

In a fit of creativity primitive man called the earth "mother" and said that she "brings forth fruits." He spoke of the "womb" of the earth. Thus he transferred the most familiar form of growth and the one closest to him into another which seemed problematical to him and which was affectively enhanced. He did this instinctively as something self-evident, because the intellect poor in experience cannot do anything but hold onto what is closest at hand or compare world-events with human things. How should a human being have expressed feelings which moved him in the face of the growth of things on earth? What should he have said? He wanted to "understand" the earth: He wanted to clarify this growth to himself. He "understood" it when he humanized it, psychologized it, when he said, "You are like me and my blood-relations." The earth and its growth moved him with the feelings with which his mother and the growth of human beings had filled him. Therefore he compared the two spheres. The analogy thrust itself on him and his world-view consisted of such analogies. This was his world-concept. It was a metaphorical knowledge, a formalistic thinking which so came to be that designations were borrowed from a familiar sphere and applied to a new, broader one. In terms of thought-economy the advantage was invaluable nevertheless, because these new vague feelings and ideas, which were crystallized and gained consistency in new symbolic objects in the guise of old words, were in fact precisely for this reason new ideas newly found. Gradually their metaphorical character disappeared from those words, and the treasure of words and ideas was automatically extended so that it became a basis for further new, realistic operations of thought.

These new expressions (every new metaphor) were created in poetic excitement—and this explains their origin as well as their character. That the metaphor contains a perceptual presentational element is only of secondary significance; essential is the fact that in it the "impulse to understand" (to psychologize) a phenomenon achieves a sort of break-through by way of association with the symbol-object. Hence the humanization of the object and the reduction of the "disturbing" phenomenon to a subjectively familiar human relationship. Sunrise and sunset—being visible—are intrinsically intuitive and plastic. Yet the poets who want to "explain" such phenomena anthropomorphically when they coin such expressions, speak in German of *Sonnenaufgang* and *Sonnenuntergang:* in describing "movements" of the sun they resort to the most common human form of locomotion: *gehen* (walking). The French speak from another equally humanizing point of view of *coucher et lever de soleil,* of the sun's going to sleep and of its waking up; thus they remain in the anthropomorphic sphere. The aspect of psychologizing, of "wanting to comprehend" by incorporating the cosmic sphere into the sphere of everyday life is even more strongly marked in the French turn of phrase. By contrast, the Roman believes that he perceives an *occasus solis,* the fall of the sun—while to the English it "rises." Thus every metaphor depends on a particular point of view, on the emotive situation, and the personal visual angle of some particular observer. The quality of the comparison (simile) is arbitrary and subjective; thus is explained the fact that in observing the phases of the sun, one person thinks of its motion, and another of sleep and awakening, and that the third in turn will emphasize the aspect of "falling" [descent].

Originally all human knowledge was "poetic," "psychologizing." Only the commonest, simplest things, implements, and skills were subject to realistic thought. Everything else was governed by similes. All objects further off were sources of mysterious, deep excitement, causes of violent emotions, activating symbolic thinking.

67

The treasury of experience was undeveloped, the distant was conceptually not assimilated, and therefore challenged the capacity for symbolization—indeed required *expression* in a similar way as the affective ideas of a poet at the present time. First of all, therefore, "expression" had to take place, the strange things had to be incorporated to the mind through comparisons. Only after the new "designations" had become familiar (that is, after their symbolic character and their feeling-accents were lost) could they become the starting-point for the reflections of realistic thought. Through the slow withering away of affectivity and through the ever-widening field of penetrating experience the sphere of poetry was gradually narrowed down and the psychologizing eliminated. The history of the human spirit is in great part that of the displacement of poetry from the world-outlook, of supplanting affects from the cosmos, and the substitution of logical analysis and objective investigation for symbolism. Poetry (which at first, in the guise of religion, myth, and wisdom about gods and demigods, finally as hero-epic, encompassed the entire cosmos) retreated, checked by realistic thinking, into a narrower human sphere. Only in the moments of basic transformation of the world-view did it recapture those primordial objects, its own original objects. Every new religious revolution instilled into it new vigor because cosmic objects again became objects of passion, feeling, emotion, and because world standards underwent a shift. An example is the influence of Christianity which proved to be fundamental in Western art, for it was a spiritually new epoch, and not only poetry, but even the plastic arts, took on a completely changed visage. The old religious task of art lay clear in view.

The Psychology of the Word as a Poetically Primitive (Ur) Element

To explain the nature of poetic cognition clearly, one finds it imperative to recur in some detail to the psychology of the word. The primitive human being who discovered the words was "poetically" gifted (i.e., verbally inventive) and, as the word was wrested from him, sensed that feeling of relief which falls to the poet's share after his psyche is disburdened by way of his poem. Originally the word, like the idea which stimulated it, was affectively accented. It possessed the double function of emotional expression and conception. Yet after longer use its feeling-content was blunted. The particular word stopped being the expression of an affect and dwindled into a pure concept—thus into a sign. Poetic similes and expressions too pass through an analogous development: They grow cold and pale through frequent use to become hackneyed phrases. This evolution may demonstrate the credibility of our theory. Through his technique the poet regains the capacity of restoring to the word its original expressive function. The particular word which has lost its expressive value cannot satisfy the poet's need of affective expression. Furthermore, his

69

nuances of thought and feeling are too complex, too singular, and too new, they exhibit too many hitherto unexpressed and therefore novel contents of consciousness, to allow him to put up with the worn-out, conventional word. They are yearning, as it were, for an adequate expression, a form. Consequently (on a more developed plane of civilization) when there exists a rich store of word-signs which evinces the fact of a more comprehensive empirical experience, *both original functions of the word* are *restored* in such a way that *alongside poetic art* that fulfills the original *expressive function* of the word there arises, to implement its purely *conceptual function, science* as a logical system of signs. These two systems of structure are, as it were, *split off* from the original word. They are a complementary development which appears at a higher level of intellectual wealth. The primitive word was a symbol analogous in power to the poetic symbol (not to a mere sign). Like the symbol-object it was supposed to reproduce and to express the idea which was in need of an explanation. It was a full-grown simile. Primitive man tried to get hold of the new idea through its sonorous expression. The sound was supposed to render the idea, to imitate it, to repeat the impression and thus to subdue it; to clarify it to the self. The sound was a rendition and a portrait. Primitive words bore an onomatopoetic character and pursued onomatopoetic aims. It was an imitation of the thing and had to be so. But even though onomatopoeia was always the aim of the linguistic effort at word-making, it could not always be its result. Only when a rendition of natural sounds was in question could the onomatopoetic attempt be crowned with full success; but hardly so when the presentation of mute objects was intended. Such a rendition might have succeeded only if those objects themselves uttered sounds that could furnish the substrate for the word-creation.

Onomatopoeia as a Substitute for Things

The success of the imitation, the invention of the word, afforded the inventor a feeling of relief. The poet achieves a revival of this original character of the word in his peculiar word-texture, but most surely in the poetic onomatopoeia.

But symbol-construction is more complicated; it is already concerned with the visual aspect of things and presupposes a richer stock of words—in short, a higher level of intellectual and linguistic evolution. The state of poetic agitation powerfully strengthens the expressive need and causes a revival of the old forms of expression. It is as if the ghosts of the ancestors began to speak again. Onomatopoeia is a description attempted in sound, and therefore a mechanical description of the object for the purpose of "its explanation." It is indeed the most primitive kind of explanation. It is a primitive medium by which consciousness liberates itself from an object when, for the subduing of the stimulus, a sound is picked which is supposed to resemble the natural sound or thing; and through this procedure the thing is "explained," understood.

One must not overlook the fact that in every single word there is a rhythmic element and that every word possesses a rhythmical inner organization *in nuce* corresponding analogously to the role of rhythm in the poetic system. Rhythm in poetry is therefore to be considered only as an extension and unfolding of the rhythmical element contained originally in the single word, a process which takes effect when a multiplicity of words has taken over the individual word's primitive function of expression.

Rhythm organizes the inspired word-masses and controls them in a mechanical fashion; onomatopoeia is a mechanical imitation, a mechanical description of the object through sound. All of these, in addition to the symbol, are the means of the self-expression of the mind. A system of expression is set up which already in sound and vibrations (rhythm) reflects the inner situation as faithfully as possible. The inner tensions and the inner turmoil are swept away through the projection of such a mental photograph: so that what was inside has now been driven outwards. But the psyche here tries to work off its distress, not by the complex, difficult and, under the circumstances, inutile method of realistic thought and causal analysis, but directly through mechanical imitation; that is, through the creation of appropriate sounds and music, and through symbols. Thus a more primitive form of thought and expression pop up again because of the excitability of the poetic mind, which now takes refuge in the primitive means of presentation and self-clarification which was once customary with his ancestors. Excitation revives the ancient need once more.

The symbolic, simile-like function and quality of the original word becomes apparent also in the fact that, for example, the first numbers used were named for objects in which the given numerical relationship was particularly clear-cut and most typically marked, so that they must have seemed particularly suitable as an expression of the numerical quality to the sense of numbers. So, for instance, the concept of the number "five" was called "hand" by one primitive people, and the concept "three" was named "ostrich's foot"—and so forth. These designations are typical as instances of symbol construction; here we face precisely that phenomenon of transference already discussed. For the relief of consciousness from a stifling indefiniteness, from dumbness, an object is brought into play through comparison as the expression of a new idea striving to be expressed.

Onomatopoeia is a paradigm of genuine sound-symbolism, of a technique which shows how to depict by a sound, how to substitute a sound for a state of affairs of the outer world—a sound which indeed is supposed to resemble materially the original. It is an explanation through reiteration, through mimetic assertion. And it is a symbolism by means of an acoustical element, as in rhythm, which also acoustically symbolizes the affective state. But the customary symbol works mostly through

73

the sense of sight, through visual associations, and it addresses itself to the intellect. The primitive word is indeed the original form of onomatopoeia, of sound symbolism. The poetic utterance even today contains elements of sound-symbolic expression. First of all, the vowels according to their different degrees of brightness and darkness possess a certain independent symbolic worth as the expression of feeling. They are indeed only the articulated and differentiated image of cries of pain and joy, as compared with consonants, which must reflect the sensuous differences of perceptivity and quality. The sound "U" [in German], for example, has a pretty dark thud and recalls a howl, whereas "A" [in German] has a considerably brighter effect. Now, the poet is not satisfied with the mere statement about an emotion in purely conceptual terms, but, driven by his need for expression, already reproduces his mood through sound —something which the primitive inventor of the word did too. Through a spontaneous array of vowels having a certain emotional coloration—thus through a sensuous sonic means, a portrait of the emotional state is created which buttresses and underscores the conceptual structure. The heaping-up of vowels of a certain kind produces a certain impression of luminosity or darkness of mental tone; whereby at the same time words sharing the same sound already for this reason prominently thrust out and engrain the minds of the audience.

The following poem by Goethe may serve as an example:

74

Über allen Gipfeln
Ist R u h,
In allen Wipfeln
Spürest du
Kaum einen Hauch. . . .

(Over all mountain-tops
There is peace;
In all tree-tops
You sense
Hardly a breath. . . .)

The two "U" 's (in *du* and *Ruh*) in close succession produce an unequivocal mood of solemnity and sadness. It is the same one which filled the heart of Goethe when he conceived the poem. The French Symbolistes, so-called, carried this sound-symbolism forward with special refinement, but consciously by design.

In rhyme in all its forms (alliteration and so forth) there is an onomatopoetic element; onomatopoeia is the true source of rhyme. This is shown also in the fact that rhyme is the most perfect wherever the verbal meaning coincides with it in such a way that rhyme occurs at the same time as word-painting and, because of its perfection, is not noticeable as "rhyme," the function it performs being double. There rhyme and sound-symbolism (onomatopoeia) are in a blend. This is most beautifully in evidence in the line of the poem cited, *Über allen Wipfeln,* which appears doubly rhymed for the

75

strengthening of the sound-symbolic element (*Wipfeln* and *Gipfeln*). And a similar blending of rhyme and sound-painting occurs in the *Dies irae* by Thomas of Celano:

> *Dies irae, dies illa*
> *solvet saeclum in favilla. . . .*

Rhyme can thus become an onomatopoetic medium, especially if it points to its origin and reaches an ideal excellence, because per se it contains a sound-symbolical element and because the repetition of syllables enhances the impression made by words so accented and increases their sensuousness, suggestibility, and plasticity. Repeatedly joined like consonants also fulfill the sound-symbolical function in similar fashion. For example:

> *Fest gepresst in seiner Brust lagen die Gefühle*

(Firmly pressed in his breast lay the feelings.) Here firmness (*Festigkeit*) and pressure (*Gepresstheit*—hard pressed) are expressed in two ways: conceptually and sonically: conceptually through the word's meaning, or rather through that of three words: "fast" (firmly—*fest*), "pressed" (*gepresst*), and "breast" (*Brust*), which also carries with it a connotation and a sonorous aspect of confinement. Sound symbolism occurs furthermore in the constantly accented terminal sounds "st." Each of these words, especially *fest* and *gepresst,* in and for itself possesses a sound-symbolic element because its pronunciation is accomplished by the pressing of the point of the tongue hard on the upper teeth or gums. The events in the world at large, the activities occurring there, are therefore reenacted and imitated through an analogous action of the organ of speech (tongue). The cumulative three-fold application of this pressure by the point of the tongue on the gums (thus the three-fold succession of the symbolic activity) invigorates considerably the sound-symbolic element which is supposed to reproduce the facts of the situation through mechanical portraiture. All of these, including the rhyme whose function was described above, are media of expression—that is, means for replacing the factual world through verbal material, through words.

The form of the poetic cognition is a result of the passions of the poet. If art is to be the authentic expression of a mental fact, its adequate replica, then the form of the work must correspond in an isomorphous way to the mental process, for the psyche achieves repose only when it has projected a structure which resembles it in terms of appearance and shape. The psyche does this spontaneously, instinctively. Here the "form" is precisely what matters primarily as the peculiar and characteristic phenomenon, for it is the form that carries the imprint of the mind even if and when the "subject" matter is in the first place the object of the personal interest of the poet. This stamp of form will constitute the "originality" ("Originelle") of the work, for in it the instinctive

77

physiognomy of the poetic personality will take on shape. Here the "what" and the "how" are indissolubly fused, and often (for instance in the lyric) the "how" basically *is* the "what." For the number of "subjects" is not limitless; they repeat themselves in the lyric and even in epic and dramatic art. But the "handling" of the actual subject is different and varies precisely as does the mental attitude of the poet toward the primordial phenomenon of the affect (love, for example), of the conflict, of the object in question.

The poet faces his object—and this is always a mental content, a mental reflection of an object at large and not the material object itself, like a mute who would express something, like the primitive who bursts forth with the word just discovered.

The realistic thinker intends not to express, but to find out and to solve (a problem). The psychic purpose of his activity is the "solution" of an "unknown," of a disturbing element discovered in a series of objective events. The thinker accomplishes this through so-called "explanation" for instance in such a way that he analyzes the "Unknown" into "known" components or in that he detects some "relationships" between the "unknown" and its environment, whereby the latter is, as it were, "curbed." As an unknown it is disconcerting per se and has to be reduced to silence by the efforts of the drive for self-preservation, which is here disporting itself on the hunting-ground of scientific research.

The thinker who pursues his "discovery" roots about

in the object-world with his sense-organs and their mechanical extensions and connects the results with the
help of logical operations. In doing this he does not abide
by the passive condition of the artist, who lies in fetters
and cries out of his mind's plight; but he adopts the
much more active (already mentioned) posture of a
hunter who hunts in the forest of objects (of reality) in
order to disarm the unknown. Not "expression," but
"discovery" is the purpose of his activity. What he is
striving to achieve is not the "presentation" of an interior
mental fact, but the "explanation" of objective "world-
particles." "Wanted" is an object, something "real," generally not even some determined particular object as
such, but as a rule a typical phenomenon representing a
whole series of objects—for instance not the earthquake
"A," but *the* earthquake as such. Obviously a mental fact
or condition may also become a scientific object of this
kind if one intends to study it like all other real objects
in the world at large.

In the instant of creation the realistic efficiency of the
consciousness of the poet is toned down. Musical images,
symbolic sounds, flow in a rhythmical narcosis, or,
rather, in the excitement which creates it; there is a
world of subjectively determined associations (similes
and symbols), a pointedly sensuous, colorful psyche with
graded attention (interest in reality); and a certain
blunting of thought-activity emerges which works more
than usually with mechanical means. It is an involution
back to the primitive. Yet consciousness does not fade

79

away. "To become aware of oneself," "to free oneself," was indeed the purpose of poetizing. But because of the psychic state of the artist, this "becoming conscious" proceeds in a peculiarly sensuous, archaic manner. And the thinking adopts the poetic, certainly the less clear and less realistic, but in return for it the more plastic, primeval form. A twilight-world evolves, a world of dim lights, a rhythmically moving world of visions, plastic images, similes, symbols, onomatopoetic effects. It is a world whose mode of association diverges from the customary one, a world in which the need for causal comprehension aimed at in the realistic-scientific exigency for the unveiling of the world recedes in face of the more primitive need for expression.

Both needs lie undifferentiated and fused in the mind of primitive man *vis-à-vis* certain objects. Yet to a higher degree than his sophisticated descendants he is subservient to the need for expression because most objects transform themselves to his inexperienced mind into causes of passions (fear, hate, and love) and as a consequence become carriers of symbolic functions. Together they create myth and religion. The pure need for expression dominates: namely, in regard to all more distant objects thus far not yet grasped and expurgated by experience. This is especially true of cosmic objects and the objects of nature. But within the need for expression, there is contained in a nuclear way the other need, the need to find out, to unravel and reveal. As has been mentioned, it takes first hold of the proximate, most immediate objects of everyday life. Later occurs the differentiation of the two needs. Then some objects challenge the expressive need, others the need for discovery, or both needs manifest themselves as two distinct intellectual structures in regard to all objects so that science splits from art. Then two self-contained systems of thought appear on the scene. This happens when the evolution of language and vocabulary as such reach a relative, material conclusion, and when realistic thought-activity in this way is already so underpinned by practical experience that it dares soberly, as "science," face the world of objects on a realistic basis intellectually, without awe, and therefore without anthropomorphic affective inhibitions.

The researcher who faces a disquieting "X" looks for its objective relations with other things, its causal links, and so forth. The poet does not assume the mental stance of a questioner. Rather, striving to express a psychic condition, he tries to "replace" it in that he imitates it by means of sound. He presents it through a sonic simile, through rhyme, rhythm, onomatopoeia, sound-symbolism, and through metaphoric symbolism. Creative of word and material like primitive man, he stays in the latter's psychic posture and like primitive man tries to express a nameless object with a sound. Like him, he wants to imitate the object with sound-stuff; for only when the similarity between object and sound-stuff seems complete, and the emotionally saturated image in this way is transmuted into adequate sound, does he become released from it.

Still, a gain in thought economy accrues through this sound-creation. Memory more easily carries along sounds than images of things; sound as mere suggestions of images are more efficient vehicles of thought than purely visual representations. Sound-construction of this kind comes into its own when the mind has at its disposal such overflowing resources of visual images and, to connect them, such a wealth of associations that it must extrude a part of those ideas in the form of sonic "abbreviations" merely as a measure of mental relief. This, so to speak, is a measure of thought economy which results from the overcrowded condition of the thought-sphere of the ego. It is emotionally accented ideas that are more likely to become objectified in this form; that is, written down in "phonetic characters," because they are most burdensome to the mind.

The Identity of Language-Creation and Poetizing

The mental balance of the poet must be upset if he is to become "word-creative." This happens for instance when a fact, an idea, anything at all, rises to the surface which clashes with an ideal, an ethical demand, with needs, expectations, with his world-view; or when a vehement wish appears. There exists, even as an everyday thing, a discrepancy between what is and what, dreamed-of and wished for, ought to be. Tragedy is a model example of this conflict. Behind every piece of writing, as a scheme of the content, there is always a "This is the way I want it to be," or an "I do not want it to be this way," an "I should like it to be so," or a "Thus I should not want it to be"—an ideal fulfilled or unfulfilled. Affirmation or negation of the content is the pattern of every literary work, acceptance or rejection is at its bottom—for a psychic content must be tied positively or negatively with the world of desires (or instincts) if it is to become converted into poetry.

If one accepts the preceding theory of art as primarily a response to the expressive need,* then the phenomenon of art falls quite naturally in line with our world-picture. The rhythmical, rhymed, symbolically pregnant (in short the "poetic") element of the literary structure is more clearly understood if we visualize the creative act of poetic art as identical with the primeval linguistic act of word-creation and if we conceive of human beings by way of excitement as being re-awakened to such an archaic type of reaction. Then man as a poet becomes a victim, as it were, of an unrestrained need for expression, as were his more primitive forebears, and he now wants to interpret the world which comes into conflict with him with symbols and to conquer it by means of "verbal" imitation, as his ancestors did. Then he piles up heaps of sound-stuff which are materially supposed to

---

* The need to say or to tell.

resemble "reality" and thereby to "explain" it. Through picture-symbolism and sound-materials a world is born which as through an act of magic replaces the real one. With the distinct clarity characteristic of hallucinations, seeing, feeling, and thinking are objectivized in sounds, tension is changed into motion, and the burdened content of consciousness is exuded outward so that it is crystallized externally in a fixed form and so that the objectified material resembles the psychic corporeally, just as a clay mask resembles its original or as one side of an equation resembles the other.

Today man's purely verbal and tonal creative phase is behind him and the existence of written languages in particular blocks the path of creation in words. The old word which through usage and attrition (that is, wear and tear) suffered a loss of its earlier feeling-value can no longer adequately express a new emotionally accented content; but frequently the novel nuances of meaning are new even in their substance; the result is that the old word has become unfit as an instrument of expression. To satisfy the need for expression, therefore, analogous, but still other and particularly symbolical, means are resorted to. The world of feelings and of thinking further broadens itself in the course of evolution so that the individual word is not able to encompass the aura of thoughts and feelings which are behind an idea or an emotion. For this reason word-systems have been built out of the primitive need for expression, systems which as structures of sound through their similarity to reality and, as symbolism, through imagistic suggestion, replace the inner world of ideas pressing outwardly, with a second world, that of art. In this order of things the original function of the word as the expression of emotion is carried over into the art of poetry, while a second complementary system evolves simultaneously which inherits (and takes over) the other function of the word: namely, the designative one as a sign now dissociated entirely from the function of the word as tool of expression. This second system—that of science—is purely cognitive. It is destined to unravel and dissolve the "unknown" in the world of objects. It therefore fulfills a practical, realistic aim, not a need for mere expression.

Logically the basically subjective nature of the poetic art results from its function as "expression." The technique of comparison and rhythmization are subjective, as is also the selection of subject matter or—rather—the compulsive force which dictates its choice. According, again, as the affect is lived down—whether its cause is described or whether the affect itself is presented—will poetic art be divided into the "objective" (epic or dramatic) and "subjective" (lyrical) branches. Still, mixed works prevail, just as in the poetic psyche too both elements shade off into one another.

If the poet becomes aware of his social role and adapts his own psychic needs to a general public desire, then his creations begin to live their own life and claim the rights of every organic structure. But its form is reshaped to satisfy the demands for intelligibility and for all sorts of reasons of the most different, be it self-seeking or social, kinds. The structures of a compulsive and unpremeditated dream-thought are kneaded in a purposive way. Too, the creation must be an organism understandable by and rounded in itself. But all of this is an act of secondary elaboration of the basic structure. This structure may indeed have accorded with an organic need, a psychic "must"; the work must be made fit for public display: a labor *ad usum delphini*.

But already the original version was vested with form and obeyed a principle of presentation—the will to present a certain sphere of thought. This will was always present and conscious in the mind of the creator during his creation even if the building-stones with which his purpose was achieved rose spontaneously from the unconscious. The creator wanted to express "something," and *this* was the lode-star of his psychic action. The creating was activity: because the spontaneity of the flow of poetic means did not exclude a zealous search for and a desire of the technical work-tools of expression. To such an extent the poetic thought-process is a true activity.

Because so much of awareness remains awake despite the spontaneity of the creation that the purpose and the object of the presentation are constantly attended to, the first "cast" is in no way devoid of logical consistency; consistency guides the hallucination even when, as a result of enthusiasm or long incubation, the poetic work bursts forth from the mind as if consummated. The period of activity precedes the "birth" of the work. Consciously and half-consciously the "search for expression" was exercised earlier, and the writing-down constitutes only a formal act. The consistency of the presentation (subordination to the purpose of presentation) is consistently completed in the secondary elaboration.

Because of his excitement out of his need for expression, the poet thinks visually, plastically, as does the child and the savage. But in mental excitement scarcely anybody is capable of abstract thought. Abstractions, which one nevertheless finds in poetic utterance are only petrifications, as it were, deriving from later epochs of thought, because the poet is creative only in the imagistic and the visionary.

The originality of the poet's world depends on the peculiarity of his experiences and appetition; they fashion the special personal character of his visions and form-creations and, through the characteristic form of his symbolism (that is, the metaphoric associations), penetrate the details of the work. The character of the poet imprints its stamp on the nature of his symbols because it creates the angle of vision from which the poet visualizes the objects of the world which he has chosen for his symbolic objects. Their number depends on his associative agility, and thus on the "wealth of imagination." If it is comprehensive enough, then most objects turn into symbols, and "emotion" conceives relationships and similarities as yet unseen. The "heart" brought them close to one another and to itself. The creation brings about an impression which is the deeper as this interconnection and cognition between the symbolic object and the stimulus-object appears to be the more striking, the more obvious, the more generally valid. If the symbol has never yet been used, it is "original." The more distinctive the feeling and the mind ("the heart and the head") of the poet (both together create the "angle of vision"), the more original his similes. The angle of vision of analogical thinking is rooted in the affective personality of the poet; it is inseparably linked with his experiences, his capacity for experiences, and is tinged with his experiences. The more powerful the intellect, the more the poet saw and felt, just that much bolder the speech, the plasticity, the association. Symbolic association possesses general validity when (and because) a certain convergence operates between the predispositions for feeling and seeing among human beings. Therefore that which becomes a symbol for the poet can also become a symbol for other people. They too can "understand" the symbolic connection. Should the presupposition of psychic homogeneity (which makes the mutual "ability to understand" possible) fail, then the work fails to be appreciated.

Rhetorical Figures as Figures of Poetic Thinking

What are called forms of esthetic apperception (whereby the word "esthetic" is misleading insofar as it could possibly mean purposive design—even some "arti-

ficial" devices designed to evoke so called "esthetic" feelings, and this would be psychologically false) and what,
furthermore, have incorrectly been termed "rhetorical"
figures—these precisely are the specific forms of symbolic
thinking. Simile, symbol, metaphor, in the first rank,
and then synecdoche (*pars pro toto*), the ἐν δὰ δυοῖν
metonymy (antonomasia), hyperbole and so forth—are
all forms of symbolic thinking. Their specific property
is always a reduction, a simplification of the thought-
content, a switch from the logical into the visionary, the
visual; the concretization of the abstract or universal;
the stress on the engrossing quality; the emphasis on this
specific quality instead of the intimation of the entire
concept, which as such is neither envisioned nor felt as
distressing. All of them reflect the state of primitivity of
poetic thought. They are the expression of the affective
vision and the emotive stress of poetic thinking. They
simplify the thought-activity; they suggest by means of a
single word a causal connection which as a result of
poetic excitement cannot become crystallized and articulated.

Let us assume the sentence: "The savage swung the
axe," where we use not a proper noun, but the adjective
"savage" in a substantival way. We do so because it is
precisely the savage nature of the subject (which does
not follow from his proper name) which explains the
fact that he swings the axe. This quality is significant for
his action and is in causal relationship to it.

If, instead of "Paris," we say *"The capital city of*

89

France was in a ringing uproar," there is a reason for the paraphrase (and it should of course be used only if it is justified). "Paris" would be abstract, not palpable, and lacking in broader perspective. But what is to be stressed is the fact that it is the capital city of France that undergoes the rebellion. The thought of the writer turns on this property of the city of Paris, not on its other functions. "Paris" is ambiguous; it is only an indication, a quite general sign, for an entire conceptual area. If one says "Paris," one can think of many things—of the great Opera House, of the location of the Sorbonne, or of an amusement-center. In the context mentioned these would not be essential. To be stressed is that Paris "as" the capital city of France, as head, focus, and center of power, is involved in tumult. The thinking (or the entire thought-process displayed) tries in a compressed fashion symbolically through this figure to indicate this "significant" characteristic of Paris—rather, the thought is not yet fully "matured" and tries to disengage itself in a symbol. But its expression remains stalled at an image, a mere intimation. An especially interesting aspect—significant in a causal or in some other respect—is singled out by means of the metonymical figure. The symbolic allusion hits the bull's eye of significance, strikes the center of importance.

Let us, using "rifles" instead of "soldiers," take the sentence, "A hundred rifles went over to the enemy." This mode of speech is supposed to indicate directly *wherein* lies the increase of forces of the enemy; that which is vital in the change of the situation is stated peremptorily. Stressed is the fact that the ranks of the enemy are increased by approximately a hundred men carrying rifles. For this reason the more concrete, visually oriented notion "rifles" is used because it applies more poignantly to fact than the general more abstract expression "soldiers," by which could be understood even the army service corps.

In the ἐν διὰ δνοῖν the substantive allied with an adjective is split in such a way that the adjective is converted into an independent substantive: for example, *patero et auro* instead of *patera aurea*. Thus in the adjective there is a reversion of type into the substantive out of which the adjectives originally came. The differentiation between being and quality presupposes a higher development in thought. At the same time, however, the use of the adjective is detrimental to plasticity, because when adjectives are used the emphasis rests nevertheless on the substantive; the adjective fades in comparison, and the quality is dwarfed alongside the noun to which it is attached. But if the original linguistic situation is re-established through a reversion to type, then both substantives shine as equivalent images. The poet therefore makes use of the dissolution (*a patera et auro*) because he was especially moved by the nonsubstantively transformed quality (*auro*), which he wanted especially to point to. But he has to pay a price because this is done at a cost of logical clarity.

Contrast sets forth two opposed (contrary) or two

common ideas in a more effective way through immediate juxtaposition or confrontation. In this way the *difference* separating them becomes more manifest, the images clearer, and the mind grasps and differentiates easier between both (contrasting) ideas. "Understanding" is expedited by the expressive device of juxtaposition. Through the expedient of appropriate (perceptually clear) grouping the mind gains easier control over the stimulus-material and the order of the successive images. Association by similarity aims indeed at something of the same kind.

In the *personification* of qualities, their allegorization into personages through forms like "wisdom" and "virtue," there is an animization of the concepts which have become objects of poetic passion and are addressed as human beings. In excitement ("if he forgets himself") a person involuntarily speaks of every thing as something animated and endowed with will, and he treats it as such. In an analogous state of mind Xerxes flogs the sea with chains. Also, a child treats his inanimate playthings similarly, because the child and the savage think of every object anthropomorphically and attribute their own essences to it. They do this spontaneously because they know no other way: If action is to proceed from a thing, then it must be something man-like: any other manner of efficacy is inconceivable to them. They cannot communicate with the world in any other than the way of speech, and if they have a relationship to any object at all, the latter will be thought of anthropomorphically.

The allegorization of qualities into the personal properties presents in addition a reversion of type of the adjectival into the objectival—a process which we have already encountered. If the mere personification of ideas like "hate," "war," "love" is adopted, the personified images retain their old grammatical gender [in German]. On the other hand, the personified qualities are felt as feminine [in German], as is also the case in Latin and the Romance Languages (for instance, wisdom, stupidity, beauty—*sapentia, stultitia, pulchritudo*), perhaps because the quality as such is sensed as feminine, as an annex of the object upon which it is dependent or as adhering to some object. Therefore substantives deriving from objectives assume grammatically the feminine gender.

But one must also notice that language attaches the article to things, therefore the qualities of sex [in German] (and even without article in Slavic, Latin, Greek, and so forth). Already in the substantive as such there is an anthropomorphic, animistic element because, even apart from sex, something life-like and man-like is attributed to things.

In every simile (metaphor)—that is, in every poetic comparison—there is a hidden grain of exaggeration which is a result of a desire to make the idea clear-cut, to "elucidate" it. This aspect appears clearly in the hyperbolic mode of language. "Heavy as ten thousand stones"; "Six wagons would have to bear that burden": The second image is even logically meaningless; its intention is to set forth figuratively only the weight of the burden. The burden which a wagon bears is heavy; if six wagons are necessary, then the burden will have to be much heavier. This must be expressed by the figure and must awaken in the reader too the desired impression, although literally interpreted it is an absurdity. Here thinking drops almost to the level of an automaton.

Now to return to the *symbol:* We saw that such an object was chosen as the symbolic object which seemed especially apposite to express a certain as yet unclear "feeling," to "explain" an idea seen from a certain angle of vision. This feeling, this idea, lacked, as a result of its uniqueness, an adequate expression: the usual current "designations" (names) are as a rule merely some general, typical indication of a typical state of affairs. Therefore the mind resorts to the symbol.

Now, what does a symbol express—for example the simile, "eyes like forget-me-nots"? A certain property of the stimulus-object. Never its entire content, but a certain special aspect engrossing to the mind—that, namely, upon which its attention is fixed. The symbol is to express that characteristic of the symbolized object for there was no satisfactory word-equivalent in the mind of the creator. In its frustration it grasps for an object which seems to fit the property which is still nameless (mute). The act of symbol-discovering is at the same time one of linguistic invention, an act of linguistic extension produced by need for expression, an extension which, however, no longer proceeds on the now atro-phied path of sound-creation, but on that of symbol-discovery.

Through the simile "eyes like forget-me-nots," the poet wants to indicate specific properties of the beloved eyes, a certain nuance of blue and certain psychic quali-ties which are supposed to be held in common by the praised eyes and the small flower which is thought of as a paragon of modesty. This connection is arbitrary and means merely the identity of the subjective impression made by two objects. But for the qualities attributed to the eyes the observer possesses no linguistic equivalent and therefore no other expressive possibility than that of referring to a symbol-object for the purpose of "illustra-tion." A similar situation prevails in every act of symbol-formation.

We notice further that symbols in the course of lin-guistic evolution have the tendency to fade in color and become quality-words (adjectives) or part of combined words where they fulfill an adjectival function (because language follows the path of concentration and conden-sation). For example, one says "palm-shape," "forget-me-not eyes," "morning-beautiful," "star-lovely eyes" in-stead of "eyes as beautiful as the stars," and so forth. This development gives evidence for the fact that the symbol expresses a certain aspect of the thing, is sup-posed to present a certain quality of the stimulus-object, and at the end actually shades off into an adjective. Such qualities are subjective in origin. They were carried from out of the feelings* into the object.

For the rest, all adjectives originate from nouns, and indeed in such a way that objects which possessed a definite quality in conspicuous measure came to be alongside a substantive in order to interpret it with this quality; and then they forfeited their original substantival primary meaning but retained the adjectival one. Thus if to express a "red" dress one says "blood-dress" ["Blut-Kleid"], the remembrance of the object "blood" may disappear and only the significance of "red" remain to the word "blood."

In a still earlier stage a human being could not distinguish between substance and quality; nor was he familiar with the concepts of substantive and adjective. A designation referred only to the aspect of the thing which had a direct emotive interest for him. When he saw a snake, for example, he might have lent a linguistic expression to his impression of it, and he may have repeated the expression when he, for instance, saw something, perhaps a branch of a tree which, in an emotive sense, reminded him of the snake. Noun and adjective flowed indeterminately into one another, and only the moment of interest found some expression in sound.

Symbol, metaphor, and simile are most intimately related. Metaphor looks like a concentrated simile or, in a psychologically more correct sense, a simile which, while

* I.e., by emotion.

hinted at, is not yet fully developed.* The simile, it is true, also grasps the object only from a certain point of view and expresses a certain definite property of it. But in a simile, the analogy is far more mature (ripened) and logically more advanced than it is in the metaphor. If, for instance, I say "the blood of grapes" instead of "wine," then with regard to certain qualities of these juices I am suggesting an analogy—namely, of the "blood" and of the "wine"—but this analogy is never fully unfolded by the explicit addition of the two members of the pair of basic concepts, "grape" and "human body." The adjectival function of the symbol is far more marked in the metaphor than in the simile. But the field of comparison, the analogical scope, is far narrower in the metaphor, however, than in the simile. It would be risky to try to fix the chronological priority of the one or the other form. It is certain that in excited speech (and one could call poetic speech the speech of excitement) metaphors gush out more spontaneously than do complete similes, which presuppose a more composed state of mind. If the metaphor seems hotter, more concentrated in taste, the effect of the simile appears heavier, more primitive. But the question of priority is of only secondary significance because both figures are only forms of the same symbolic thinking.

In a series of metaphors we have seen the anthropomorphizing tendency of metaphor, the transfer of the

---

* It may be also—on the contrary—an abridged simile.

concept out of the familiar sphere into one requiring explanation, the projection out of the human everyday life into the cosmic realm. The world has been psychologized.

Besides, we find metaphors like "sharpness of thoughts" and "softness of heart" in which certain real characteristics, technically very familiar phenomena, are transferred into more complex structures to make them more concrete and intelligible. Tactile experiences (like those above) are projected into mental and intellectual functions for the purpose of "elucidation." Feeling and thinking are illustrated through simple sensations of touch (soft and sharp), and herein precisely lies the comparatival, the symbolic element. The proceeding betrays the effort of the mind to explain the new and the complicated through the old and the simple. Here also belongs "the milk of human kindness," in which a sense of taste is called upon to depict psychic qualities.

Let us analyze a symbol: The poet Zuckermann was moved by his war experiences to write a poem whose first stanza goes approximately thus:

> *Drüben am Ackerrand*
> *hocken zwei Dohlen,*
> *Sterb' ich am Donaustrand?*
> *Fall' ich in Polen?*
> *Was liegt daran?*
> *Seh' ich unsre Fahnen weh'n*
> *in Belgerad.*

(Over there at the edge of the field
two jackdaws are crouching.
Will I die on the banks of the Danube?
Will I fall in Poland?
What does it matter
if I see our banners wave
in Belgrade?)

In the second stanza instead of jackdaws there are "two ravens," and in the third "two crows." In other respects too parallelism prevails among the stanzas.

The "two jackdaws" are a symbol. The poet wants to express his melancholy—and jackdaws are not on the edge of the field, but on the border of his mind. These symbolic animals symbolize the presentiments of death rising in the poet, as the third line shows. The blackbirds are thoughts of death projected outwards. The image is of course not original; the associating of jackdaws, ravens, and crows with death is ancient. The analogy of birds and thoughts is pertinent because thoughts usually rise to the surface and disappear quickly. That human beings use precisely these blackbirds as death-symbols may be grounded in the association by contiguity. They dwell on battlefields and fields of corpses and busy themselves with carrion. In addition, "black" in itself passes as a color of grief and death. This color-symbol can perhaps be derived thus: Death is saturated with fear so much because it seems to be the dark, the inconceivable, and the unknown par excellence. But in life there is still another situation which fills archaic human beings, and today children also, and many nervous grownups with a similar dread: night, which lacks light and is dark. But at one time it was also the most dangerous part of human life. It must have severely frightened nomads and earlier human beings who had no tents. At night they were far more helplessly than by day at the mercy of lurking enemies, animals, and nature, who were invisible. Fear of the night must therefore be present atavistically in human beings, particularly since in civilized periods night is also more unpleasant and perilous than is the day. Death and the unknown have pursued human beings more by night than by day; night was the bringer of death, and therefore black was death's color. And, besides, human beings represent the state of death as black—namely, wanting in light; and for this reason this color is attributed to death.

But the second color of death and sadness is the exact opposite of black—namely, "white." Instead of "dying" one also says "growing pale," and the pallor of dead people and perhaps also the growing pale of a living person present at a death may have caused the association of the white color with death. "White" is therefore also "bloodless"; people growing old and weak become white, and even when nature is "dead" in winter, snow lies on the earth. But death is also cold like snow and ice, and both of these are white in color. These components may explain "whiteness," the color-symbol, as the color of death and sadness. The color-symbols of "life," by contrast, are "green" and "red." (Another set of associations makes out of white the symbol of "purity." Furthermore "white" may be the euphemistic contrast of "black" and perform the latter's role.)

Let us now return to Zuckermann's poem. If one reads it closely, one will sense in the resignation with which the poet awaits death something like longing for it. The jackdaws are far-off, at the edge of the field; the border expresses distance and at the same time a desire for these distant creatures. But they are not reachable: they crouch on the border. The number "two" must also attract attention. There are "two" jackdaws. It is always a risk to follow up the arabesque-like path covered by an association; still the number "two," which appeared intimately wedded to death and longing, perhaps conceals an erotic phantasy. (Perhaps the poet longs for death of the two of us?) Love and death always go together. In the transport of love there seems to be something of dying. (Certainly it is a death of consciousness.) It is also recognized that love eagerly unites with thoughts of escape, going away, disappearing. And the desire to go away and to escape has something of a longing for death; it is the desire, as it were, to "put to death" life as it has been up to now.

The symbol "interprets" an emotively stressed and not clearly outlined idea; it lends it an "osseous framework," a "contour," which it previously in its vagueness lacked. Thus it lends "words" to the mind, helps it to achieve a clearer self-understanding. Nevertheless, it must remain ambiguous, polyvalent and complex because the idea which is at its base is not simple, but complex, and presupposes a whole array of implicit ideas. In the symbol-object a whole multitude of ideas is lodged which in condensed and compressed form rise into consciousness through the symbol-object. The symbol-object usually represents a not quite clarified, composite and not fully matured idea, which reaches out for consciousness. In a sense, it is a consolidation of this complex idea. But it yields only one "facet" of the idea, one "quality," precisely the one emotionally impinging on the mind.

5

*Symbolic Thinking as an Archaic Phenomenon:
Animism, Infantility, and the Naïveté of
Poetic Language*

Symbolic thinking is a more ancient, archaic form of
thinking; symbolic "explanation" is an older form of the
need for explanation. Analytical, scientific interpretation
does not, as does the symbolistic, try merely to transfer
familiar words and images from one sphere to another in
order to "explain" the latter; rather, it examines and
analyzes the object itself in order to reduce it to simpler
elements; in symbolic thought, however, the stimulus-
object is "explained" in terms of ideas, and also linguistically, merely through a simple psychological act, as it
were mechanically, in adducing an alleged analogy and
achieving thereby a soothing of the mind, and solace.

Language has grown by way of the extension of words
of particular meaning into new facts; and as a consequence, the outcome of symbolizing, objectively speak-

ing, is nothing but an enrichment of language, which nonetheless does not bring with itself any emendation of our knowledge about things. It is merely an enrichment of our expressive capacity for mental phenomena. The presupposition for this mode of thought is a lowered ability for the examination of reality, as it were a blurred, almost enchanted form of vision. Today the poet fails in this examination of reality because of the ecstasy into which an emotional disturbance transports him. The primitive neglected it out of naïveté and actual poverty of experience, and, beyond this, surely also out of inner excitement, because only the latter could release the need for expression and thus stimulate the invention of new words and symbols. It has been medically proved that children, and also the insane, from whom illness has withdrawn the power to distinguish dream from reality and the ego from the world, possess an unusual inclination for making symbols and are thrown back into the archaic form of thinking which the poet also practices— of course because they cannot as yet, or can no longer, resort to realistic thinking. But what is a natural level of development in a child, who mentally retraces the course of its ancestors, becomes reversion in the poet and in the demented, except that an emotional disturbance (poetic excitement) kindles the process in the one and illness does so in the other.

Poetic language is animistic. It demonstrates a regression of the poetic psychic mechanism into the animism of primitives and of infantilism. Lifeless things, plants or their parts, are treated with cries, praises, and curses as if they were creatures equipped with will and endowed with moral nature. Occasionally a "sympathetic" nature appears as if it had understanding for the emotional states of the agents in question: cataclysms, thunder, and miracles accompany the death of the hero. The poet is "superstitious." He often sees "portents" and takes "panpsychism" for granted, not of course theoretically, but as a matter of fact; and in insignificant events he "sees mysterious connections" between a fateful and knowing will and the personal experiences of his creatures. But human beings find just this world-form, the "earlier" one, pleasurable and "beautiful"; it corresponds to their "ideal," their mental "need." It is the world of youth and of the youth of mankind, and it therefore answers to "feeling" and thus to wish. It is a world of desire.

In poetic discourse abstractions take on the form of deities and living minds (exactly as one would "wish" them to be); they become personified and animized. The animistic pattern of symbolical thinking has already been stressed. The "world-view" of the creative poet is anthropomorphous. He has returned to the archaic thinking of his forebears, in terms not only of form, but also of content. If he carries on a "dialogue" with a fir-tree, an animal, a forest spring, the sun, and the stars —when he "treats" them as human brothers—he regresses to infantilism and to a primitive state. But just for this reason his work is found to be "moving," and it "pleases."

The use of diminutives already shows this. For example, in the passage from Claudius:

> *die goldnen Sternlein prangen*
> *am Himmel hell und klar*

> (The little golden stars sparkle
> brightly and clearly in the sky)

the stars are addressed as children through the use of diminutive endings, and the "childlike" engagement of the poetic psyche to the stars is manifest. In general this childlike attitude expresses itself in this, that the inanimate objects assume the character of members of a family, as it were; and the relation of the small child to members of the family represents the model of the affective relationship of the naïve poet to objects of nature—an approach which corresponds with that of primitive man in relation to the universe.

And what has been called the poet's intimate sense of nature, his as-if-it-were innocent intimacy with all mundane entities, is precisely the naïve treatment of natural creatures as human beings, as living minds, with whom one chats and complains, so that forest and flowers, and all of nature, seem to vibrate with living beings. "Dame

Nightingale" and "Mother Nature" are two terms which demonstrate the animistic and (again in terms of the example of family relationships) the anthropomorphizing feeling-state of the poet. This intimacy with and childlike feeling for nature may have been aroused in the poet by a strong passion, great pain, or an unusual sense of happiness.

It has been indicated above that animizing and humanizing the world brings it closer to the human heart by transforming the mute world into a social being, thus producing a sympathetic response in the enjoyer of art. The animistic and animating view of the world is deeply rooted in the human being's habits of thought, and answers to his emotive needs. For him the mechanistic ("scientific") view of the world is a disillusionment and a condition to which he first must, but cannot, become reconciled. That he is alone in the world, in a world made up of a combination of mechanisms and atoms, is a thought which to his mind is an object of horror. He feels himself surrounded by a world of strangers with whom he has nothing in common. Precisely because it is childlike and primitive, the animizing outlook appears so touching. It suits man's wishes most of all; it is his "innate" and natural view. An animated world is an old habit of thought and a human being's deepest wish. This kind of thought enchants the hearer and reader into a desired world, into the illusion of a loving world kindly to man, and transfers him for brief moments into an enrapturing dreamed-of land, into a child-land, into childlike naïveté, into the bliss of the child's psyche, for which the surrounding world has not as yet assumed the rigid, mechanical, and therefore humanly alien structure of reality. It is the land of the hour of prime, and a human being loves prime just because it is prime and agrees with him.

Such wish-fulfillment brought about through poetic form by the poet's reversion into an earlier stage of development, that of far-away ancestors and his own childhood, for which heredity, habit of mind, early experience, and inner desire created the predisposition—such wish-fulfillment secures bliss for a human being. It is of course a reversion into a world of desire: thinking without effort, freedom from the control of reality, passive existence drifting along, consciousness not burdened by remembrance, not laden with reflection, freedom from the pangs of an ever-present memory, an untrammeled life, a primitive, primordial existence, a thinking which does not yet distinguish between beings natural and human, but "passes over" the distinction and poetically changes the world into a blood-related family of minds.

The sense of nature is animism and means nothing but an animistic attitude toward the world. Those passages and dicta in poems which are said to be "true" and to come from the "heart" when they refer to objects in nature betray an animistic attitude toward the world—for this attitude answers the demand of human nature for social intercourse and mutual understanding. Basically a person understands (and also longs for) only beings and actions whose motives correspond to his own. Only one world-order, that governed by psychological laws, seems to him "understandable" and "explained," and is also "desired" by him. Every other explanation, being alien and non-anthropomorphous, leaves behind in him a residue of dissatisfaction. Therefore the deep satisfaction brought about by those poems in which the naïve animation of the world is manifest. Those passages which show an intimate, direct, and, as-it-were, almost corporeal communication between human beings and natural objects seem especially attractive—passages devoid of reflection in which the social (love-) need toward the world-being is evident and the *willingness* to understand turns into an *ability* to understand, so that the individual believes himself to have wandered into a garden of human-like beings.

In the moment of greatest agitation, the attitude of the poet to the world is fundamentally animistic and anthropomorphic. It is expressed in its purest form in the lyric by Claudius:

> *Der Mond ist aufgegangen,*
> *Die goldnen Sternlein prangen*
> *am Himmel hell und klar;*
> *der Wald steht schwarz und schweiget*
> *und aus den Wiesen steiget*
> *der weisse Nebel wunderbar.*

> (The moon has risen,
> the golden starlets sparkle
> brightly and clearly in the sky;
> the forest is dark and silent
> and out of the meadow rises
> white mist wonderfully.)

Characteristic of the poetic mind is the exposing, the laying-bare, of the most secret desires in a primordial, naïve form, coupled with a stripping-off of the conventional. It is an exhibitionism *sui generis*. Living human beings never speak to one another as do poeticized figures. They would do so if they had the courage of truth, the courage of their instincts and their thinking. But social laws overwhelm them. Even people in love cannot succeed in speaking as does the poet, who lends them the words. This directness of feeling, this uninhibited expression of wish and desire startling in its truth, is an infantile trait. The stripping-off of conventional shame and the disregard of social usage is childlike and primitive. The emotion washes away the social superstructure, and there follows a lapse into the shameless freedom of the child and the primitive. About this the person enjoying art feels the same elation as he does about all other symptoms of childhood, because in a human being there always remains, as in a dream, the need for an unfettered existence. Its realization for him means a wish-fulfillment; and everyone wants to return to the land of the fairy-tale. Most of what we call "the heart's desire," "the demands of feeling," and emotional needs (and therefore the postulates of the affective structure of man faced with the world) is basically a need in a human being for an epoch long past for mankind, a yearning of his "older" archaic heart. And—as to its contents—it is at the same time essentially the wish to revert to an "earlier," a "previous" form of existence.

Childlikeness and what it recalls animates the soul with that earlier condition which is devoid of struggle, conscious reflection, and the social consideration grafted on only later. It is a return to an unfettered state of freedom so appropriate to it, to a state of tranquillity, to a state of relative impassiveness which is consonant only with a child living in the present. This spiritual state has an ease relatively unburdened by memories and ideas because it resembles a flowing series of sensations rather than the unrupturable painful chain of memories culminating in unremitting efforts. But lacking also are the moral inhibitions set up as watchmen before every desire, the entire structure of the ego which inescapably holds a human being in check from maturity until death. In the poetic world lies the unending relaxation carrying with it freedom from inhibitions. It is the return to a childlike sorrowlessness of the past, to the unveiled expression of feeling, to the state of infancy. We find charming and beautiful this transplantation backwards into the archaic state of youthful freedom, of fairy-tale-like animation, of twilight without effort. It is the return into "once upon a time," into the sheltered security of mind. And this is the ideal, the yearning, and the wish of the individual; it is also identical with the wish for deliverance which is nothing other than the wish for turning back, for home-coming, for a return to childhood and unconsciousness.

Furthermore, the erotic attitude of the poetic mind seems archaic. Poetic art is eroticized and indicates more intensive occupation with sexual contents than is usual in actual life. The greatest part of fiction is nothing except a variation on this one theme. The power of emotion released by the sexual drive may first and foremost be prone to awaken in the poet a need for expression. Yet it is unusually significant that sexuality has exerted an uncommon power over the psyche of primitive man also, a far greater one than over that of civilized individuals, because its ubiquitous sway over the life of man declined in the course of civilized living. But it still rules in the realm of art and still dominates the psyche of the poet with unrestrained native force.

6

*Poetry and "Criminality" or the Power
of Emotion*

We must now undertake an examination of the relationship of the poet to an archaic phenomenon within society
—that is, to crime. It is generally known that the poet
turns toward the criminal with sympathy and pity.
Poetry of all times is a battle-ground of extraordinary
passions. All crimes of passion—incest, adultery, prostitu-
tion, murder in its most varied forms (infanticide, parri-
cide, and manslaughter)—are the objects of poetic interest. Fraud in the "heroic" shape of treason up to forgery,
even theft, challenges poetic explication and transfigura-
tion. In view of the intimate connection between form
and content in poetic presentation, this can be no acci-
dent. For the content calls forth a particular form. If the
poetic interest turns toward the sphere of crime and the

world of the outcast, then such interest must be based on the psychic organization of the poet.

The criminal is a human being who pushes aside the confines of morality and indulges in the satisfaction of his drive or his egostistical need. When he risks an immoral deed, he reverts to the distant time in which barriers to self-satisfaction were raised neither by conscience nor by law—to an "uncivilized" time in which every man did as much as he was able in the direction in which he was driven. It is the time in which children still live today. One must not believe that then a person could have indulged in blood-frenzy. He satisfied himself only as often as he was powerful enough not to have to pay attention to a barrier erected in his fellow-beings' interest. Children and animals are still on this moral level even if (only in exceptional cases) do the latter become cannibals of their fellows in their own species; but they do not shrink from any struggle in case their interests—always hunger or love—push them into conflicts. They are unbound. Their drive knows no limits. Renunciation is alien to them. It is brought about only by constraint. And an inner restraint rooted in conscience, which ultimately appears in men, is not yet developed in them. Moreover, inner constraint and renunciation are, both of them, the offspring of reflection, and presuppose pondering and conceptual thinking.

The criminal is a person whose self-seeking drive in one or another event succeeds in the face of inner bars and who hopes to escape the outer one, the fist of society.

The drive is stronger in him than is the inhibition. Here a regression of will, an involution, occurred in epochs of unfettered impulse. Indeed, it is asserted (by advocates of the milieu-theory) that not a "predisposition," but social relationships (need and similar factors) produce the criminal. On the other hand, one must point out that the milieu comes into question only as the factor triggering criminality. True, thieves in the technical sense exist more frequently among poor people than among millionaires, because committing burglary or plundering a safe holds no fascination for the owner of a castle. Other, more lucrative, but therefore not the less objectionable, ways harmful to society are open for his greed. He satisfies in another way his criminal dispositions rooted in his egotistic lust for power and riches; all people by virtue of atavism possess criminal tendencies, even though of different intensity. If these did not exist in the psyche, a person could never become a criminal, or a tyrant, or be addicted to violence, despite milieu and opportunity, despite want and occasion, just as a deer never becomes a carnivore or the lamb a lion. If the drive is to break out, the predisposition must exist. If the occasion, the need, or a conflict of interest supervenes, then a person in his aboriginal primitive nature is ruthless and, obeying his urge, a thief, a murderer, or a cheat. Among the affluent the criminal impulse (that is, unvarnished ruthlessness) avoids the crime of burglary, and assumes the more sophisticated form of fraud, or has its fling through plots and machinations in the realm of politics. In Shakespeare's plays about kings and in his tragedies, a preoccupation with criminals comes clearly to the fore.

Sexual life remains a further stage of human brutality. Here the egotistic impulse celebrates true orgies, and there are few people who would not be privy to deception in this realm. All social classes without exception rove on this hunting-ground, and as a result of the power of the sexual drive, the power of self-indulgence in this respect is so great that the immoral is not forbidden here either in general or in any form. Therefore the English saying: all is fair in love and war. Thus the realm of love is likened to a field of battle, and the evil-doer in it is exculpated in advance. Yet such conditions are felt to be disgraceful, and the extension of the moral law to the relationships of the sexes to one another is demanded.

According to everything so far said, the criminal disposition, amoral unrestraint, can hardly be regarded as an exceptional case. It manifests itself in all people, though in different intensities and not under the same circumstances. It has not once been settled that this tendency is of greater force in a criminal liable for punishment than in a blameless person. For the latter, occasion or need may have failed, and his drive may not have taken a path typically tabooed. In many people, particularly in those of extraordinary will power, it may appear more vigorously pronounced. In those endowed with a vigorous drive, a minimum of external circumstances will suffice to stimulate the natural tendency and to effect the regression of the individual's will.

Exactly as the so-called human desire for sensation—and thus the pleasure in preoccupation with criminal themes and events—obviously results from an affinity between those greedy for sensation and criminals—which might explain why those subject to the vice of sensationalism are shamefacedly loath to admit it; so must the fact be found in the psychic organization of the poet that the products of poetic art are full of acts which in bourgeois life pass for crime and have to do with the representation of human beings who are criminals according to the law. The poet does not treat of subjects which are psychically indifferent to him. He is touched to the quick by what he artistically formulates and projects. In order to arouse his poetic interest, things which he presents must be alive in him too. Intuition primarily is rendered possible by a psychic identity between the presenter and the presented. This correspondence can be initiated through compassion or hate; but one also cannot avoid the question: why the compassion? Why hate? Surely only because it concerns things with which an affective relationship exists in the poetic ego and which it must present or overcome, affirm or deny. A great poet has asserted that in him there is the possibility of every kind of crime. The possibility may inhere in every man, except that he is not aware of it in the same degree because he is less tortured by a need for expression.

Now, if in the course of this consideration it was stated that poetic form of presentation means an intellectual regression which results from the emotional emphasis on the contents of the poetic thought, then it must be further established that it is just these stirrings and propensities which occasion a break-through of the primitive in the feeling-world, and to a great extent cause that intellectually regressive kind of representation. The nature of the impulse which causes a regression of the will stimulates the mode of representation which presupposes a regression in the process of thought. But affectivity sticks most stubbornly to such egotistical impulses because they are linked most intimately with the life of wish and instinct.

Poetic interest transcends the realm of the "criminal" and the erotic as an inspiration for the poetic presentation. These subjects do not exhaust the world of emotions. Nevertheless, the interest does not extend beyond the range of objects emotionally involved.

But if we try to clarify the interdependence of the field of emotions and the poetic mode of presentation, then the following consideration might be in order: the emotional disturbance removes whole strata of thought and conjures up an archaic thinking-activity in which the components of realistic thought float around, as it were, as ruins and remnants of an enlightened epoch of reason and furnish the building stones, the elements, for the archaic thought-activity of the poet.

The emotional disturbance itself, however, is also a

primitive, almost a prehistoric phenomenon of mind. The development of civilization leads toward the repression of the emotional outbreaks; the immanent ideal of evolution aims seemingly at enabling human beings to face events with the equanimity and composure of the initiated and the experienced. A layer of intellectuality screens and shrouds emotion. The ever-so-often felt awareness of the nature and of the genesis of affect-laden ideas, the illumination of the causes of feelings, blunts emotion and destroys a part of its formerly uncanny virulence. But it still keeps hold of a large realm, the realm of art. And it too aims at the conquest of feeling: through expression.

Knowledge is a powerful regulator of the feeling-life even if the latter in its primitivity constantly tries to free itself from the former and to revert to the past. The saying about people who are "sicklied o'er with the pale cast of thought" has its source in this practical psychic experience. The developmental direction of the individual takes the same part. Emotionality recedes in confrontation with intellectuality. This is not merely a development in the direction of lassitude, but a mental advancement which repeats itself on a much broader scale in the mass-history of mankind.

The primitive person was a creature controlled far more by emotion than the civilized man and subject far more to strong emotional shocks. For him the world was overflowing with possibilities for violent emotion. His inexperience, the naïveté with which he faced natural events, and the uncertainty of his existence subjected him to storms of passion which a person of today is able to elude. Natural events, once the objects of fear or terror, today glance off people without effect. Understanding rules feeling-life and transforms it; at least it tries, even though with varying results, to determine its development; and wherever one can observe a continual change or permanent change in the emotive-life in the course of human history, it is traceable to knowledge as the creative motor of evolution, to a changed world-view and a changed world-experience.

But besides natural events, the events of social life and the vicissitudes of fate have lost a part of their effect as factors generating emotion, although a person's virulence has more refined feelings and has at his disposal a more widely ramified and a more differentiated wealth of feeling than in the remote past. As a result of the influence of the intellect, of knowledge, however, he seems to a lesser degree to be a victim of the impetuosity of dark, powerful, and, in their irrationality, enthralling emotions. He comprehends the inevitability and the causal connection of the events; he wants and is able to do so. The attrition of the immediacy of feeling-resonance, the damming up of outbreaks of feeling, and the restraining of the predominance of irrational passion increase according to the degree of intellectuality. Despite the fact that the stock of feeling always becomes richer, powerful emotion grows infrequent, more of a prehistorical phenomenon which breaks out from time to time. The occasions for it become scarcer, however, and only strong, deeply rooted needs and overpowering revolutions draw it forth.

There is of course a province of feeling in which the dominance of emotion still remains relatively unbroken: the sexual; the intractable sexual drive with difficulty accommodates itself to the colorless world of civilization and gives evidence of emotions of unusual power. This drive too is repressed, and the strength of emotion here too has declined. Relatively seldom does one directly and forcibly satisfy his carnal desires with a woman who pleases him, as did occur in primitive times. There may be a tendency in this direction—otherwise the law to prohibit it as offensive would have no reason to be; but this tendency must have declined because otherwise it would not be forbidden. An impracticable law remains without effect; also, humanity cares to issue only such laws as are consonant with a social interest and the observance of which is attainable to its psychic powers. For example, deceit in love has not been forbidden, except when it has occurred under especially qualified, hazardous circumstances, because humanity knows that otherwise it would be forced to transgress the norm every day. Yet the power of emotions exhausts itself even in the sexual sphere, and reason sallies forth even here.

But by emotions one must not understand merely the powerful welling up of feeling outwardly perceptible and coming to the fore. There may be emotions not entirely conscious, furtive ones, which originate in more or less clear ideas and which, though outwardly not perceptible, possess a greater dynamic power than those which are manifest. These suppressed and not completely conscious emotions are surely the more productive poetically. Similarly the after-effects of a manifest emotion remaining in the mind can become the source of poetic production.

If one has once grasped the emotional disturbance as a primitive phenomenon, as a regression, then one can more easily understand precisely why it is destined to cause poetic, equally regressive thinking. The primitive element in the world of feeling levels thinking and drags it down to itself. Feeling as such beclouds thinking, anthropomorphizes it, and suffuses it with fantasies and wishes. Thought must be free of feeling in order to become fully adequate to the exigencies of reality. Otherwise in place of the cognitive need, the need for expression erupts with the described accompanying phenomena breaks out.

Thus there is a parallelism or interdependence between the world of feeling and that of thought. The world of feeling, if reverted to its original "emotional form," produces a more primitive condition of thought in which the need for poetic expression tends to appear. This begins to burgeon as often as "feeling" invades the world of ideas.

7

The Chief Characteristics of Poetic Sentence-Structure: the Rustic and the Primitive

At times country people speak like poets. Their word oftentimes is as pithy and to the point as the poet's because, as a result of lack of education, they look for words to express their thoughts without making use of the usual stereotypes. The originality of their speech contains something awkward. It is a search for expression. In poetic speech too there is something at times thick-set and circumlocutory. The poet's tongue almost has something clumsy about it. Excitement has robbed him of language, and he struggles for expression so as to make the reason for his excitement clear and to defeat it. In order to achieve clarity, therefore, and accomplish expression, he struggles for the image, for the rescuing symbol, for the simile. Sometimes one hits upon repetitions of stanza and word through which consciousness lend stress to the contents or alleviate words. But at the same time there arises the impression of an awkward, rustic thinking which rehearses the passage two or three times in order to make itself familiar with its significance or to come to terms with the subject. Something of the mode of discourse of the uneducated is manifest. But all that seems compulsion or deficiency in the poet is transmuted into the palpable and plastic in his work: the lack of precision of his ideas is transmuted into symbolism and the agitation of feeling into rhythm. The primitive person speaks plastically in images, in symbols; the modern skeptic with precision, with conceptual but colorless, almost ossified, signs.

In poetic discourse the principal clauses prevail. Subordinate clauses are kept in check. This results from the eruptive and passionate nature of poetic thinking. Violent emotion has stifled logical transitions and left only eruptions of thought. Only the outlines of thought remain; only massive mental images pass through the subtler transition of the thought-processes; offsprings of a later development in language, the connections of logic which slow down the flow of images, are wiped away. Excitement does not tolerate them, but creates a more explosive thinking built out of sensuous images and disconnected quiddities. A reversion into a less complicated, more massive thinking has occurred. The eruptions, the symbols, disengage themselves from the vision and pursue one another. A causal connection of members of the representation will be sought in vain; but such a connection was never intended either. Something internal has to be reset and expressed in something external. This is a cinematic kind of thinking.

If, as has been mentioned, scientific thinking is oriented causally and is directed toward the analysis of the object and the discovery of connections between it and the environment, toward its decomposition into simpler elements, as is also reflected linguistically in a chain of principal and subordinate clauses; then here (in poetry) only the need for expression which is to be satisfied. But this is secured in such a way that the subject-matter is mechanically mastered through musical formation, through the supply of adequate sounds and a succession of sound arrangements, through the creation of suggestive imagery, which ranges two ideas according to the principle of an emotively distorted analogy, but not through positive cognitive achievements: not through a rooting about in reality and a dissolving of it into cognized elements, all of which can even be later verified experimentally as to its factual correctness.

During poetic creation realistic thinking undergoes obfuscation. Association by similarity as we see it in its creative function in science is paralyzed; instead, the association by contiguity and a symbolizing analogy adulterated by emotion dominates because it is not really reality that is to be known or analyzed, but an agonizing idea that is to be expressed. Crowding symbols and images pour forth and liberate the psyche. The idea puts forth sounds and sound-sequences, and the rhythm mirrors the tempo of the emotive movement. Causal connections are not sought. The "revealing" of things is not attempted. In general little is inquired about and more is asserted. "Attention," the orientation in reality in order to unveil it, is lacking. The "will" is stifled; images, supposed to "explain" stream forth, compulsively yet freely, to "explain." It is through objectivization that the mind attempts to free itself of agonizing ideas. It therefore constructs with mechanical means a structure which is supposed to present, to surpass, and to replace this world of ideas. The child in his speech-effort and primitive man in his linguistic innovation make use of the same method and for the same (expressive) aims. To that extent it is a regressive phenomenon; for it is not the attempt at expression and the linguistic effort subservient to it, but the search for the real which is "timely" and which stands on the "apex" of contemporary evolution. The symptoms of regression therefore appear immediately in the symbolic character of the thought-process, in the reawakening of animism. Thinking becomes animistic and anthropomorphous. A positive act of knowledge does not succeed.

Yet this animistic imagistic thinking, because it suits the older levels of consciousness and indeed answers to the childhood of the individual and the dawn of humanity, grants deep satisfaction to those enjoying it. The mind snugly falls back into its comfortable past, with which its thought-habits and its feeling-needs agree more than they do with rigid realistic thinking dependent on attention.

Poetic thinking serves the creator's need for self-explanation. And it is not the "desire for the comprehension" of reality in the realistic sense that is intended here, but a desire to understand which is satisfied and which "understands" only when these ideas find an adequate expression—that is, by means of the poetic technique, the mechanistic and anthropomorphous invention of imagery, and so forth—and, indeed, only then. These phenomena of objectivization free the mind of the dark contents of its ideas and satisfy it. Powerful excitement lends its specific character and its characteristic coloration to the medium of expression, and this need for poetic elocution is identical with the archaic need for linguistic expression. The completed expression which constitutes conscious awareness affords pleasure.

Poetic technique serves the need for expression and for consciousness about oneself through rhythm, which groups and controls the sound material by way of the automatism of repetition. It lulls the emotive agitation to which it owes its own origin into tranquillity, through symbolism and a verbal technique supposed to reflect "faithfully" the contents of the ideas. In this connection it must be stressed that "poetic technique" is an unconscious technique, an instinctive technique, of our mind. Basically it is nothing but an "adequate" mirror of the emotional state and the emotional content, except that the regularity and the typicality of its occurrence gives the impression of a "technique."

To be sure, the poetic need for expression born with and issuing out of emotive agitation contains a "need for explanation" which in some way is connected with the impulse for knowledge and really includes it. Nevertheless the agitation has already influenced the thought-activity of the poet, and the subjective interest in the stimulus-object has blinded him to the "problematical" and typical in his particular case, to the extent that no investigation of reality on his part can succeed and could not satisfy him either. Rather, an eruption of the stimulus-content toward the outside for the purpose of psychic discharge is to take place: therefore the sonant means of the emotive reaction of a mechanical kind, the rhythmic structure of the subject-matter which matches an inner agitation, and the invention of symbols as the visual component of thought alongside the above mentioned acoustical ones—all of which are a portrayal of the mere external face of these ideas. All "empty" means of a mechanism of sound and vision, which are at the same time the media of a primitive mechanism of thought, are the deployed which are supposed to compensate for the ideas, to countervail, to replace and conquer them, instead of stating them. It is the mode in which the mind wants to get hold of an oppressive content in order to cast it off. The rational grasp of connections of fact or of causal relationships, of the analysis of reality, is not even attempted. Also, it is not objects themselves which must be portrayed, but rather the imprints which they leave behind in the mind, their psychic profiles. This "mechanical" activity of thought and explanation temporally precedes the realistic type. Because of an emotional excess, the mind cannot ascend to the higher, super-individual, scientific type of thought. But it is precisely this incapacity which becomes the source of artistic pleasure for the votaries of art.

Poetic consciousness is a deeper tuned, a more darkly colored type of consciousness more closely related to unconsciousness. Still, it remains a form of consciousness sufficient to eject the crowding feelings and purge them, and to transform the unconscious into speech. Poetic symbolism and imagery by themselves already embody sensuous-plastic attractions and values of tone and color which turn up before the retinas of art-enjoyers to produce a feeling of pleasure apart from and in addition to their inherent expressive values. Owing to the properties of poetic style, they sink the mind into its deeper infantile layers, into the animistic world of desire. The visual and acoustical values are accompanied by a lowering of the level of realistic thinking which "returns home" to its primitive state while the rhythmic elements "counteracts" the mentioned aspects of sensuous splendor by a musically polishing and leveling of the entire utterance, by dampening the sheen of certain light-values, by evening out the realistic and the thought-like, in order to rock the mind to sleep and lull it into security in the stream of uniformity. But the characteristic double function of rhythm manifests itself in this, that through its mechanism of group arrangement it facilitates the mastering of its contents for consciousness, but puts it to sleep by way of uniformity. This duality of function permeates the whole of poetic thinking in other ways also— as thinking it serves the mind awakening to unconsciousness, into a state of repose. This state is created by verbal expression, by a suggestive arrangement of sounds whereby rhythm plays the tranquilizing role of a uniform pendular mechanism. But if the inner content of agitation is deflected to the outside as rhythm, then tranquillity must remain in the inside itself. The function of rhythm is also comparable to a cradle which puts the child to sleep through uniform motion. This function has deepseated physiological roots.

Poetry, like every mass-creation of intellectual humanity, goes through a development which sometimes repeats itself in miniature in the mind of the poet. At the beginning of the evolution of poetry, the realistic elements are scarce in lyric poetry, and in the "pure-bred" type of poetic thought, in the lyrical poet, they are like petrifications of a "later" epoch, chance erratic boulders in the poet's mind. Here the means of poetic technique are intrinsically the most fully marked, in word-and-image symbolism, in rhythm, now and then also in rhyme in its primitive forms. But the further development is characterized by a decline of the purely poetic elements testifying to the ecstatic origin of poetry. Slowly a rationalization of poetry takes place. Rhyme and rhythm are the earliest to wither away. But the remaining evidences of poetic thinking too deteriorate. Poetic ecstasy cannot any longer prevail in the *details:* it becomes overgrown with the complicated contents and a realistic thinking growing stronger—with the prose of a complex existence. An approximation to the usual (realistic) type of thought and description (narration) establishes itself. The visual factor, the intuition anchored in symbol and simile, proves to be more tenacious, but in the naturalistic drama and novel even this gives way. But as a whole symbol and simile still remain true to their origin and their task.

A rebound and a vindication of old poetic rights of the psyche succeeds only after a renewed strong convulsion of the spirit of mankind, and therefore also of the individual mind. The prevailing world-picture then is being destroyed, and so is the unstable equilibrium of the mental world-view. In such eons world-understanding is revolutionized, and, as a result, the mind of the creative artist is shaken to its deepest instinctual foundations, so that he again has to roam the world with song and symbol in order to recover it. Yet, as has been indicated, there is always present in *all* poetic creations, those of naturalistic prose not excepted, one origin, one face, and one common task: such creations are always visions, replicas of an emotive individual content, and the expression of the poetic mind, its liberation from agony and not world cognition, is the common aim of all of them. No phenomenon is ever conceived as a typical individual case to be realistically analyzed, dismembered, and reduced to simpler elements after which the life of human beings has to adjust itself to such findings with the help of technology. All of this would be the task of science, which might be able to proceed in such ways toward the creation of concepts of a higher order, toward the classification of phenomena, toward the discovery of "laws", that is, recurrences in the phenomenal world. But this is not the task of art, not even that of "naturalistic" art: art is not an achievement of knowledge; it orders not the world, but the poet's own mind, which "tells about" (expresses) itself and in this way is "assuaged."

The artist's mind throws the formed material of representations to the outside as a mimetic surface, as a portrait, as an imitation of mental contents, as their substitute; it objectifies the imaginative material, transforms it into sounds, transforms the internal into the external in the struggle for self-liberation, and accomplishes an act of emotive mastery, self-purification, and the attainment of self-consciousness. This creation is never hyper-individual, even if it is *valid* for *others*. It cannot be an analysis of reality, an arrangement according to similarities for the sake of cognition. A mental copy of an agonizing state of affairs is to be put forth, and in the form and outline proper to it in the mind—not in a drawing, which is the method of the scientific observation of reality.

In the world-evolution of poetry, the prevailing element of the poetic (in which are floating like flotsam and jetsam the newer, realistic components of thought) gradually retreats, and the flower of poetic symbolism slowly degenerates into rudiments and relics of a former splendor so as to give way to a drier prose-utterance. In the same way a similar change occurs in the mind of the individual poet. As he grows older, the element of reason always becomes stronger, and the writer of lyrics becomes a writer of epics or a dramatist. Or the ability for creating poetic form may simply dry up. Then the power of poetical association, pregnant with symbolism, weakens and the specific excitability withers away.

I have attempted to explain the style and technique of poetry as organic products of a mental state and a psychic need which grow unconsciously, compulsively, and automatically, even though for the teleological observer and for the conscious writer they are degraded to mere method. I discussed the working process in the creative, poetic genius, in the true originator of poetry. The conscious imitator who has learned how the poet works was not taken into consideration. Virtually, the poetic "streak" may exist in every man, though in unequal intensity; but the amplitude, the originality, and the power of the true poet are missing. Imitators and poets of lesser breed use the means of the poetic style as conscious work-instruments of proved effect. Even the true poet, supposing he is conscious of his gift, may equally know how to manage the poetic ability as a craft; he may then employ it without being driven to it by inner necessity—just as there also exists sexual intercourse without love, eating without hunger, and other realms of automatism.

Much has been said about the "blending" of the sexes in the poetic psyche. Now, it could seem probable that whatever links the poet with primitive man may also constitute a bond between him and woman. Yet the poet *struggles* with the unconscious; a struggle which is a masculine trait. But this struggle does not transcend an individually determined need for expression and presentation, which may be ascribed to easy excitability, and the latter may be due to a feminine component. Qua action, the poetic form of reaction is masculine, but insofar as it, as a result of his sensibility, has to remain a merely expressive reaction and cannot either rise into science and the superindividual or be transformed into something "active," it may be due to the feminine tendency. The ecstasy which makes a poet of a poet can be thought of as feminine. And it is also noteworthy that women have shown more substantial achievement in the realm of poetry than in other spheres of intellectual activity. I have already mentioned the strong erotization of poetic thinking. As I have demonstrated, this presents a characteristic archaic feature; it presents no less a feminine one.

The image of the poet which has been disclosed to us by a study of poetic form agrees essentially with the one construed by the instinct of nations and the observation of generations. We are clear about the "madness" from which the ancients already derived poetic art, and about the naïveté and childlikeness of the poetic character, about which many stories have been told. The source of poetic creation out of the unconscious has been revealed. But we also saw that a minimum of poetic ability dwells essentially in everyone, and we dared to look for the springs of poetic art in the primitive instinct for language, to find its source in the need for expression which originally included also the need for knowledge and which the poet still follows in the creative instant. But we should like once more to state that the poetic vision, poetic associations, and the capacity in this direction are purely intellectual. The poet is indebted to an intellectual superiority for his faculty of vision, for his power to perceive analogies and common properties; on this superiority every other creative, particularly scientific, associational gift ultimately depends.

8

Artistic Achievement and Artistic Enjoyment

If one is to be clear about the bases which arouse esthetic pleasure in the person who enjoys the poetic work of art, one must fall back upon the principle, already mentioned, of the mental identity between him and the artist. The art-work is the expression of the poet's world of desire and feeling. If this feeling-world is identical with that of the connoisseur—that is, if the same attitude toward the world animates both of them so that similar psychic complexes within them are in need of expression —then esthetic satisfaction will appear in the devotee of art if the "expression" of the poet was so successful that it was able at the same time to portray the mind of the enjoyer of art.

The "excellence" of the work depends on the striking mastery of the world of the representations of the creator: on adequate reproduction of his sphere of symbols and the true recurrence of the heart-beat of feeling in its rhythmical equivalent, the verbal mass having been enclosed properly through word-music. The "mirror" of the mind must be to the point, and it can then also be the mirror of other minds. The depth of the impression of the work conforms with the depth of the mental strata reached by the symbol or the "symbolical personae" of the work, the deeper the impression of the work. Through appropriate symbolization a deep cut, as it were, uncovers the contents of the mind. The symbolic being then does not only express impulses gliding on the surface, but also at the same time the deeper, more secret ones, so that representation of hidden and early desires and "thoughts" are represented and the appreciator, moved, stirred, and set free, finds that the content of his silent depths is expressed.

The consumer of art re-experiences the process of expression in the poet, and it is important that the energy of the poet's violent emotion and his stock of images is absorbed in a series of symbols and musical values because the psyche of the consumer partakes of this "archaic" form of liberation which is pleasurable for him too. And what has freed the artist by way of objectivization delivers him also. The more truly music and symbolism express the spirit of the creator, the deeper his mental strata able to reach upwards, through them the more complete also is the self-liberation of the consumer and that much more intense is his esthetic satisfaction.

The minds of human beings are filled with an ever-lasting, always alert, passionate longing for expression, always unsatisfied and unruly as is only mankind's incli-nation toward reproduction. This need for expression is constantly swelled with receptivity and ready to put all objects of the world into use as symbols in order to achieve self-satisfaction. The mind forever hungers for expression (self-representation). Language, poetic art, sculpture, and music serve this hunger. Yes, even archi-tecture and landscape perform only the function of ex-pressing the inner world for the soul. It is given only to the artist—and to nature—to fulfill this need for expres-sion ("to tell what he suffers"—Goethe).

Values of color and tone and arrangements of words can claim esthetic value only insofar as they possess the symbolical and expressive function for the consciousness —insofar as they are symbols and serve as objectiviza-tions of an idea. To an African a symphony of Bee-thoven could precisely be a series of meaningless noises, just as *Hamlet* could be a heap of unintelligible individ-ual words and empty images. Necessary, therefore, is an agreement of psychic presuppositions if the poet is to be understood by the appreciator. Consequently, the de-mand for the "identity" of the mental world of the artist and of his "disciples" is certainly valid.

Symbolic objects are subject to change in space and time. They vary with "world-feeling." What at one time is a beautiful simile need not remain so always. Today no one will say, "Your nose is like the tower of Lebanon which looks towards Damascus" (*Song of Solomon* 7:5). In the present the rapture of love no longer reaches this point; nor does it even in the Orient. Thus one cannot experience it any longer; he can only feel it vicariously (if one transposes himself into the mind of such people —which is not difficult because a "disposition" to do so may be present). On the other hand, the expression "forget-me-not eyes" is meaningless for a Bedouin. This also explains the oscillations of taste in art, certain difficulties in "understanding" the products of other cultural spheres, and the failure to understand novel art-works.

But no object, no line, no color, no tone intrinsically is unable to become a subject of symbolic or expressive value. Every object, every perception, possesses an immanent feeling-value; something in the mind agrees with it; and as each appears, it evokes a feeling-response and "represents" something.

Thus in summary I should like to say that the art-work possesses expressive or presentational value—that is, esthetic value—for the receptive person because the consumer finds himself in an analogous disposition to that of the artist who has created the work, which disposition, by virtue of its affinity, then procures for him the expressive or "liberating medium" for his slumbering mental substance. This affinity, and hence a general "receptive readiness," exists in most human beings because their minds generally are in need of expression, so that the potential or actual psychic identity between creator and enjoyer, the ideal inescapable condition of "understanding" among persons of like or related cultural groups, seems universally given per se. In such a manner for the enjoyer the art-work means the fulfillment of an inner want and a release from an unconscious world of a silent anguish, as it did earlier for the poet. It is the word which is given to those who are speechless.

9

An Interpretation of the Beauty of Art and Nature on the Basis of Poetic Thinking

The esthetic of poetic art provides a basis for the judgment of esthetic feeling in general. When one sees an architectural or natural object, a feeling of pleasure may result from the contemplation of the external shape—thus of the "form"—of the thing. Usually we then say that the thing is "beautiful" (and this is indeed the most general term for esthetic judgment).

To explain this phenomenon, one finds it advisable always to be mindful that those structures of poetic art are "beautiful" which with completeness "express" certain internal elements—thus which "correctly" represent the mind, because one can surmise that not much else can be true of architectural or natural objects.

Now, why are these objects, a human being, an animal, a landscape, or even merely a geometric figure, "beautiful"? What do they "represent"? Why is a partic-

ular building valued as "beautiful"? Does it also represent something? First one must guard against confusing
the concepts "beautiful" and "purposeful" and similar
terms. That a building is purposeful is the practical *sine
qua non* of its usefulness, and probably also the presupposition of its being called "beautiful"; but usefulness is
not identical with beauty. Certainly it is absurd to build
a railway station like a church and a villa like a factory.
Nevertheless, so perversely planned a building, could,
despite its absurdity, be pleasing in terms of its shape
or form, and thus could be beautiful. For when I look at
the façade of the Pitti Palace, I do not think of the
purpose for which it was built, of what is carried on
within it, or of whether it is a castle, public housing, or
an office. The building would be little suitable for public
housing because that runs counter to its original purpose; but the arrangement of the façade might continue
to be beautiful notwithstanding. On the other hand, one
cannot tell why one must worship Zeus in a temple like
that in Segesta, Sicily; one could just as well do so in a
hut, a grotto, or a building crowned by a cupola. But the
Greeks acted differently because such buildings are not
merely "purposeful structures"; and their shape is not
only a function of some use and of the technical know-
how of the Hellenes, but also the expression of some
kind of world-view, a representation of wishes, ideals,
and aspirations which found their realization precisely in
this form of temple only.

One calls a building "beautiful" if it outwardly exhibits a certain meaningful arrangement, an agreement of the parts among themselves, and certain proportions which have an esthetic effect. It must therefore by itself possess, even in a pure geometrical sense, a certain pleasant form, so to speak. It must thus have an inner "harmony." What is to be understood by this term "harmony"? First, organic order in general, organic order in and for itself; and also the "correct" organic order. It must be a "reasonable" structure too, one which can be "grasped" at first glance. It must exhibit "proportions" of its own, as does a living "sensible" being (without excrescences, unfitnesses, and exaggerations), as does an organic creature, as does—when all is said and done—the human body, whose form constitutes the ultimate unconscious model.

And of what does this "harmony" in a purely geometrical sense consist? In the repetition of a certain element of a geometrical nature. And this repetition plays exactly the same role in architecture as does the element of repetition in the rhythm of poetic discourse. If short or long, accented or unaccented, syllables are repeated, so in architectural "harmony" certain geometric figures, lines, and structural elements are repeated. The repetition of equal elements—the repetitiveness, which is precisely what constitutes the inner order (the organicity) of the "form"—remains essential. Therefore one may call static "harmony" a quiescent rhythm, and rhythm itself a dynamically swept harmony.

The ordering of the material, whether rhythmical or

otherwise, in itself endows it with "meaning." The ground of pleasure in the organized object lies in its easier controllability by the mind. The material by these means assumes an "organic" shape consonant with consciousness; it becomes a "being," as it were. The mind, which itself is something confined and formed, has a horror of the chaotic and has a need to mould the world-stuff it grapples with into "enclosed" structures in order to grasp them and to shape them into organism-like, self-similar wholes. Thus, through the repetition of elements inherent in a structure, we can achieve its "definiteness" and hence its "intelligibility." The latter issues into assuagement and "sleep." The mind understands and realizes the structure at a glance. Its "significance"—that is, the law of its life, its construction—becomes clear. At its sight the mind has an inkling of and "looks for" the formative hand—the "form-maker."

But inner "harmony" dare not degenerate into monotony, because if it does, the advantage of the formation is lost, and the numerical and rhythmical are again dissipated into the chaotic and limitless. Pleasure originates in perspicuity because it has proportion and is measure, because as such it exudes "meaning."

This purely formal beauty of a structure, and thus its rhythmic order, which makes us grasp it in view of its commensurability, does not exhaust the entire mental contents of esthetic satisfaction. Basically, the same pleasure accompanies the contemplation of a geometrical figure, a circle, an ellipse, a rectangle, a square, or a meandering line. Neither mere speculation nor empirical inquiry is able to decide if a circle is more "beautiful" than an ellipse. Now—although the circle was considered more "perfect" in the past—the ellipse may be superior to the circle because it is a more highly "organized" structure than the circle and therefore is also able to "express" more than the circle. On the same basis, an octagon may be preferable to a square. In these structures, rhythmically superior because more complicated but still perspicuous, the human mind discovers more easily a formative will. Thus the figure of a star can appear more beautiful than a triangle. It seems more to be "being"; it "expresses" more; it represents more. But here we shift our ground to the second factor which makes up the esthetic quality, to the "symbolic value" of every structure—that is, to its expressive value for the mind because of its "meaning." And every line and every geometric figure possesses this symbolic value. It "means" something to the mind.

It does indeed express something obscure. Therefore it might be possible to explain why—apart from the purely technical differences of craftsmanship existing at any time—different epochs and different countries exhibit differences of shape—i.e., different geometric basic forms —which they prefer to other equally available forms. The preference for one geometrical basic form over another may have primarily a technical, but also other, reasons because of psychology and world views.

The prototype of a building is the cave-dwelling or its

artistic derivative, a "box" provided with an opening. But how this box is shaped depends first, on the technical knowledge of the master-builder, and second, on his mental needs—thus on his ideals. People of the South in Europe preferred the square and afterwards the round forms of building, whereas in the North the triangle appeared in much greater diffusion as an element of construction. The temples of Greece are based on the rectangular forms; in Rome the circle came into its own. The Flavian Amphitheatre (Colosseum) is round; so is the interior of the Pantheon. In Byzantine buildings the circle dissolves into a half-circle, and the half-circle is further divided, and so forth. This fact has reasons not only technical, but also spiritual, reasons rooted in the mental need for self-representation.

The new form must express a certain spiritual yearning, realize a certain desire. Such a principle as functionalism (purposefulness) can explain neither changes in style, nor, for that matter, any style as such. Stylelessness too is a style and expresses a certain attitude of mind. Also, a person who asks for the "purely functional" only postulates an ideal and will create a "style," one among many, which seems functional to him but less so to his successors, who will by no means acknowledge it as purely "functional" in an absolute sense but consider it as one ideal of form one among others.

If the architect becomes a "creator," he shapes his material not exclusively according to "function," but in a

146

form taking his fancy—thus in a manner which expresses an emotional need. The psychic values which are in need of expression and strive for representation are sometimes difficult to define because, just as the contents of music, located on the boundaries of the domain of concepts, they are difficult to translate.

Lines and figures as such have symbolic and expressive values which, however, become more explicit in a completed structure. The Taj Mahal and its environment are expected to connote a quiet sorrow because buildings chiefly express the ideals not only of the architect, but also those of the owner—and thus of the period. The Basilica of St. Peter and its square, ecclesiastical structures, in their forcefulness remind one more of antique-Roman greatness than of any secular structure in Italy; power and grandeur here were to be expressed with enrapturing elegance. Today no one would venture to destroy so venerable an edifice as the old Basilica of St. Peter. For a new building one would instead look for a different site. This modern "conservatism" also betokens an ideal.

The round structure of the Flavian Amphitheatre is certainly not the only structural form fit for the performance of gladiatorial combats. But in its powerful proportions, in the form of the frame, was to be represented an urge and a posture of those who commissioned it. Likewise, there are round and angular campaniles whose practical purpose always is the same; but the appearance of a building does not depend only on its purpose; nor does it depend only on "tradition," which after all does not explain change; but it does on the frame of the spiritual attitude of the builder, whose mind craved for an image.

Thus it can be said that the form of a thing also possesses—*in addition to* its formal value, i.e., its intrinsic "rhythmical" worth—a symbolic value as expression. There is the added further fact that every *content* of a (formed) thing also has some "significance" for the mind, and therefore a "meaning." For the mind it functions as a symbol of something psychically important, and therefore as an expressive value.

Every naturally grown object and, even more, every landscape possesses a natural "beauty." These objects awaken esthetic satisfaction insofar as they fulfill their intrinsically organic law. A birch-tree pleases as a birch-tree; one does not require it to look like a cypress. There are gnarled and slim trees: the gnarled ones seem beautiful when they fulfill their intrinsic law of gnarled-ness, the slim when they fulfill the law of slimness. The olive-tree is beautiful in itself when it looks like an olive-tree. Every creature is self-sufficient. The same thing exactly is true of animals. They must show their natural proportions and thus fulfill the law of their kind. The elephant must not look like a lion, or the lion like a squirrel.

The same applies to landscapes. A high mountain chain is beautiful, but a hilly country of green forests has a beauty of its own too. Yet according to what principles does a person "choose" between trees and animals, landscapes and figures? Primarily according to the proportions of its arrangement. In general the formed object is sensed as superior to the unformed or the less formed, and, indeed, because of the greater "potential for expression" which is inherent in the more formed as compared with the less formed. Just because of its superior "variety of form," it may express more spiritual contents. As the star is to the triangle, so will the luminous star be esthetically preferable to the colorless one. Therefore a high mountain landscape will in general be deemed more pleasant if it reveals "beautiful" summit-structures than will a "monotonous" high plateau; and a pinnacled high mountain-chain composed of forest, rock, and glacial scenery generally will be estimated as more beautiful than a merely naked rock-formation, and so forth. But such appraisals are of limited value because these components of form may have a different importance. In addition, the "contents" of scenery in view of their symbolic pregnancy play an important role in esthetic judgment. "Taste" changes: that is, according to the ideals and worldviews of human beings, a type of landscape will be approved in one epoch, and then later people will be indifferent to it because it no longer expresses ideal wishes. There were times in which the taste for high mountains was slight (despite their overriding "form value") for, according to mood and world-desires, human beings find satisfaction in mildly waving hills at one time, and then, later, according to what they want of the world, in wild chasms. In this connection nature becomes a means of expression and representation for the mind, just as does the word. It is a silent utterance, as it were.

The same principle would obtain in the esthetic judgment of individuals, animals, and plants. The expressive potential inherent in the form of the cypress may be superior to that of the olive-tree; nevertheless one can find more pleasure in an olive-tree than in a cypress or a palm-tree. A person who loves wise Odysseus more than brave Achilles may find more pleasure in the olive-tree than in the cypress. And to an ardent young man a palm may "say" more than does a fig-tree. (It expresses his soul more.) A human being who loves large forms, power, and strength may take more delight in a lion than in a squirrel because the lion expresses his yearning rather more. Someone who loves daintiness will prefer the squirrel with its agility and coquettish tail, which reminds one of a beautiful flourish in a signature. Women are in general more attached to cats, men more to dogs. Here too an ideal and an elective affinity express themselves. About the symbolic value of forms one could also remark: a human being unconsciously prefers those forms esthetically which in their proportions, but not necessarily in size, approach the proportions of the human body; and a person relishes more the form of a lion rather than that of an elephant, which is an archaic creature rather strange to our world and which therefore appears strange—a fact, which does no injury to the "symbolic value" of the elephant, however. I believe that for a human being the elephant among animals seems to express the "wise old man." Thus it is not surprising that a person takes "our" world of forms as the measure of beauty because he also classifies the degrees of skill, agility, and power of a creature when he compares them with his own.

A tree bearing blooms can be more pleasing than one without blooms because the expressive potential of the being "tree" increases when the color of blooms is added to its greenness. The arrangement of the shape is enriched by the arrangement of colors; and in the color as such there is an inherent symbol-value. New expressive possibilities for the mind appear through coloration. But these are exhausted neither by shape nor by color; the symbolic value of growing and blooming must also be added, and this value carries into the representation a certain longing, certain desires, and ideals. The symbolic value of the "contents" of a natural phenomenon as an expressive value of the mind must be considered if one is to describe the entire extent of esthetic satisfaction. Thus one must also "understand" what this natural phenomenon "means" in order to exhaust the sphere of pleasure it is able to offer.

We bring along certain emotional demands, certain ideals, and consider ourselves satisfied in the face of natural and architectural objects when they are expressions of wishes and ideals. Therefore monotonous objects

—for example, deserts, seas, and prairies—although inferior as to variety of form to other types of landscape, may yet afford pleasure to certain people or to people in certain moods, precisely when the monotonous or the boundless make up the object of their yearnings, and constitute a symbol for them, an expression of their minds. And this is also true of colors and lines. Even though the expressive potential of a "colored" figure surpasses that of a colorless one, a merely linear drawing can nevertheless be more "pleasing" when the very line by its duct represents a striving for expression because color could work only in a "disturbing" way and blur the symbol. The "beauty of content" is thus shown to enjoy priority over that of mere form.

This is true also in the area of human beauty. To be sure, one can also say that a human being, supposing that in his proportions he fulfills the law of his type and race, must, like all natural creatures, be esthetically satisfying. But this is not quite the case because an ideal postulate and wish—a factor which overwhelms the "pure beauty of form"—deflect esthetic judgment. And what is called ugliness can scarcely be determined only by a mathematically definable deficiency (too short or too long, and so forth) because we would in that case always remain in the realm of the "formed"—thus of mere "form." Form too is operative. Yet, as soon as we speak only of "regular" or "irregular" lineaments, we already *ipso facto* admit that we have in our minds some kind of ideal image which we submit to phenomena in order to compare them with it. But, apart from "regularity" which, we are able to note in anticipation, could in this case be some kind of average ideal of a race, a further element toward clarification of this "ideal image" must be referred to. The mere outline of the traits alone will not be decisive. Its "pattern" will not always be a model of mathematical harmony. Other factors contribute to carve out the ideal image, particularly because a human being also chooses between two equally beautiful or equally ugly objects. This choice is determined by other already-mentioned factors alongside the "rhythmical" presuppositions. This applies to landscapes and to human beings as well. The ideal of beauty changes according to epochs and even according to days. One generation shakes off what the preceding one admired. The Renaissance ideal of women is not that of the rococo, and that of the present time has nothing of both. The ideal fluctuates according to individuals and regions; changes in taste may be well traced in works of painting and sculpture. Today even the Venus de Milo no longer better supplies a feminine ideal.

Thus, the harmony of proportions is not decisive; the "contents" of the object decide the choice—the emotional relation to the contemplator, the symbolic value of the form-contents as expression of the desires of the enjoyer. We must return to our starting-point: every shape, every line, every object of human activity, earthly architectonics—whether architectonics of nature or of art—is, or, rather, becomes a picture of mental contents, a sym-

153

bol, to the human being who looks at it or fashions it. And indeed not a simple symbol, but, like all symbols, a many-layered one. For the colonnade-circle of Bernini does not express only what it is supposed to express directly, but, beyond this, what every round form presents as such. And this is very much, even though it is something "indefinite." Every form recalls more or less remotely the human or a natural body or a part thereof. These bodies or their parts possess expressive value and are symbols to the mind. Every line has a representational value as does the poetic word.

Every line and every shape at the same time represents objects, recalls in some way objects which possess psychic "value," expressive value for the observer, "mean" something to him, and reproduce forms of feeling—accented objects or memories of them. Form, lines, colors possess "meaning"; they represent something from out of the mind; they are the objectivized containers of some thought, of some feeling, and express something as do words. This is the writing of the world which man reads. He reads it as if it were a writing made for him, so that he could find in it his own incarnation. The world with its forms is really a simile to men (Goethe) —namely, a simile as the expression of his inner world— the description, the face of a spiritual, psychical element.

A rectangle, a triangle, a circle, an ellipse indeed possess a varied expressive potential; nonetheless it can become difficult to set up a valid hierarchy here. But when entire peoples prefer the triangle and others the circle as basic structural forms, the reasons are mental. One could say that those with a "masculine" ideal of beauty prefer the triangle, whereas those with a "feminine" ideal of beauty select round structural forms. In general roundness appears more pleasing and more graceful than the angular, and this might also have sexual reasons. For man is the creator of esthetic ideals. The round line awakens numerous connotations linked with the round forms and the suppleness of the female body. Roundness passes for "soft," the pointed and rough for "hard." The preference for the round form could be so explained that, in the round structural forms, wishes and ideals (of femininity, mildness, and so forth) find fulfillment. But the celestial bodies—sun and moon—are also round. In this connection one may also not neglect the purely technical side of things. The straight lines of pointed forms are more easily drawn and presented than are round ones. The evolution from pointed to rounded forms stands out clearly in the plastic arts, in architecture, and so forth. Rebels then start once again at the beginning.

At times, the Corinthian column might have expressed more correctly the ideal of beauty than the Doric one. It also perhaps has a greater expressive potential and as a symbol is richer in expression. Its trunk, tapering toward the top, has more life, resembles more closely an organic being, human limbs, an arm or leg, or a growing tree. The Doric column is less "articulated," more primitive; its expressive potential is slighter perhaps; the Corinthian as a symbol is more equivocal in meaning, more allusive, because not only in its "articulation"—that is, in its form and rhythm—it is superior to the Doric one: its round, smooth, lithe line awakens memories and stimulates the "imagination" more; it expresses more.

Everything that is, is also a symbol. A line, a color, a tree, every natural phenomenon "means" something— that is, it serves the mind as an expressive medium of its psychic contents; it therefore is a symbol or an object of comparison. Besides, a human being indulges in an instinctive pan-psychism as a result of which he senses every natural phenomenon as if it were a production of "architecture," as an emanation of an anthropomorphic will similar to human will. Considering any natural phenomenon, he asks how it was "made," what it "signifies," and he conceives of it as a "work." For him the natural object therefore possesses an inherent "meaning" for which he looks during contemplation; if he finds it, he is inwardly gratified as if by a building made by someone like himself, because he has "understood" it as an essence related to him; as an emanation of a psychic being. And only for this reason can the natural object become a symbolic object, an object of comparison for his psychic phenomena—thus a tool of expression; because the human being apprehends these natural objects pan-psychically and anthropomorphically as an emanation of an anthropomorphically psychic being.

High, snow-covered chains of mountains arouse moods of power and grandeur in human beings; and the same is true also of large, well-proportioned temples with huge columns and simple, but powerful proportions. That is to say, the human being involuntarily conceives of mountains as of something "meaningful," as the "architecture" of a spiritual will. He compares himself with the maker of this work and thus feels obscurely that the builder of these mountains in making them wanted to give expression to a desire for greatness, as, for example, he himself as human being would create such works if he wanted to create something great. But at the same time he feels that his mortal powers do not suffice for the creation of such mountainous beings, and concludes that the psyche which extruded out of itself such mountains was uncommonly powerful; he conceives of the mountain-chain as an expression of the power of its modeller, and finds in the same mountains, as in all architectural work, an expression of his own longing for grandeur. Thus the mountains become a symbol to him, they please him as a "symbol," and they "mean" something to him. It is a structure psychogenic and therefore pregnant with meaning, and it has become so because it was perceived as a carrier or as a creation of a "will."

To note something already mentioned: that in the object the "beauty of content" takes precedence most of the time over "beauty of form," thus over rhythm. A less regular beauty may "please" better than a regular one, assuming that it is more an expression of an ideal for the contemplator. Someone may therefore feel a great esthetic joy in an old, crooked lane and in an aslant building than in a boulevard or in a temple, because the former "mean" something to him and are therefore the embodiment of an ideal.

Calm lakes evoke certain aspects of thought and feeling like peaceableness and sweet melancholy because a human being would have constructed such a landscape if he had looked for an expression of sweet melancholy; and for this reason precisely he finds expression in this natural phenomenon for his moods (after he instinctively has conceived of them as an emanation of something psychic).

Thus, all world-objects have their sphere in the mind as if they were creations of an architect. But an animal will hardly be able to have an esthetic experience: it does not "understand" these phenomena. To it they are not meaningful emanations of a psyche and cannot become an expression of thoughts and feelings, objects of comparison, and symbols. The animal as it observes them thinks nothing; thus no esthetic feeling is aroused in it.

The brook and the stream have their "sphere" in the mind. A narrow mountain brook "affects" us otherwise than a broad stream because a man would create a stream in one mood and a mountain brook in another mood. Therefore they "mean" something different to him and express something different. Every natural object is an embodiment of an idea slumbering in the soul, as it were, and struggling for expression, or, rather, an expression of a psychic behavior, an object of comparison. And in our case one could say that a human being would start a mountain brook when he is a child and a stream when he is an adult man, and that the spheres of feeling are determined by such psychic factors according to which he feels about "stream" or "brook."

A person's psychic behavior expresses itself in language too. Man imagines everything that is as the expression of a psychic behavior of an organic state of affairs. One speaks of a "stormy" sea and a stormy heart, a calm sea, a calm mind. Such bodies of water are stormy or calm—apart from meaning "dangerous" and "not dangerous"—only for one who imputes a psychic behavior—namely, an inner "quiet" and "unquiet"—to the elements. "Objectively," things will nevertheless so behave that the most unquiet sea (inwardly) will be more quiet than the calmest man. Here we have to do with the projection of a psychic state into an object which can never be the subject of such a behavior. Consequently, the transfer of the term "quiet" or "unquiet" to the sea is entirely senseless because it assumes something psychic in the sea. In the expression "quiet" sea, therefore, there is a buried simile: namely, the human being is compared with the sea.

This too is pan-psychism. Men animize the universe and treat things as beings or as products of beings. Thus one projects the content of his ego to the outside, speaks and acts as if he were not only the measure, but also the model of all things. What he calls large and small is so only in comparison with himself, with his works and possibilities. He transfers rest and unrest, characteristics of his mind, to elements, compares them with himself, and finds in them the expression of his ego. As he uses such psychoid expressions (like rest and unrest) he thinks about his state of mind, his mental condition, his fate; he thinks of these elements as if he abided in them: that he were quiet on a calm, unquiet on a heavy, sea; that his pulse beats more quickly and his breast heaves more vigorously when he is in danger; that he would have to be as violently excited or rushing (or would have to love noise) like a child if he were to run like a mountain brook.

He calls a heavy sea unquiet, and this unquiet sea awakens in him feelings which arise in him when he is restless and stir up that entire apparatus of ideas which causes such feelings—strength, anger, or an otherwise great violent emotion, with its background. The heavy sea is a simile, a symbolic object; it represents certain psychic contents and presents them; *through its appearance,* feelings are expressed and ideas depicted by words. It functions as "expression": namely, as it were, as a "sculpture," destined for the liberation of the mind from ideas; it is also an objectivization like a statue and a building. For the psyche it therefore plays the role of a work of art.

For a human being the world is a writing, a picture-writing, an object of comparison for his mind, an expression of himself. And when it becomes this and because it becomes this, it affects us "esthetically"—to the extent that it can also become expression, the release of the mind from the oppressive shadows in its innermost self, and the fulfillment of its desire for expression. For the mind, things too have expressive value, value as an anodyne and release, and the more the obscure emotional material is released through the world's symbolism, the more it is objectivized in those things, the calmer does the mind become.

This emotional satisfaction will become the more intense, the more the observed object is fit to express the individual feeling-complex of the observer, the greater the affinity between his psychic contents and this object seems to him to be. A person yearning for greatness may be pleased by the high masses of mountain chains, rough-lined and angular, because they "mean" greatness and express his desires; thus the landscape becomes a formal wish-fulfillment, a redemption, for him. It satisfies his longing for expression.

Although monotonous desert wastes and endless steppes cannot be satisfying as models of form, lacking diversity in form as they do, they may nevertheless afford some "enjoyment" to a man who is in great sadness, as, for instance, may cracked pillars also, because they express his soul. He longs for dissolution and a chaotic infinity which bring about death-like weariness and torpidity of vision. He sees a wished-for world before him. But such moods may affect anybody. The landscapes in question may provide at least "some" contentment for everybody. The same is true of every content of nature. It may happen that a man demure, full of grave thoughts, or in pain appreciates and enjoys an idyllic landscape or a musical pastorale because his pain has not yet risen to the wish for self-destruction, although he desires a world of peace. For one desires not only an increase of what he has, but also such things as he misses most. This is an example of the mechanism of contrast. Rousseau believes that one could describe freedom the most beautifully in a prison.

During the rococo period a cultural ideal was developed whose embodiment is to be seen in the paintings of Watteau, and this was in contrast to the gravity of the baroque, by which men were clearly bored. The "line" of the rococo was related to that of the baroque as an arabesque is to a meandering line or champagne to a heavy Southern wine. And the predecessor of the baroque line was the more severe line of the Renaissance, with its rectilinear components, which seems more masculine and more chaste. Changes in such tradition of lines proceed very slowly. Lines have a great tenacity.

Women who pleased the people of Watteau's time certainly did not conform to the taste of the antique, Hellenic period; the Greeks had other desires, because they had other ideals. The female-types of the rococo were formed by the education and the mode of life derived from the cultural ideal of the rococo. The world-view created a (psychic) idol; this was moulded into the living body, and pleased. But those dainty forms could not have caused any esthetic satisfaction to a peasant, who did not share this cultural ideal, except as a matter of longing, *lege contrastus,* or as matter of respect —that is, admiration—for the higher classes, who, as a desired type, also may have become his ideal of beauty (therefore the *"idéal des mains branches"*). Indeed, the slave usually has as his ideal of beauty, not that of his race, but that of his masters, therefore that which is longed for by him, as for example (in times passed) that of Negroes in the United States.

The ideal of beauty changes with the world-view and the emotive attitude, but also according to race and class: but in such a way that the subjugated often have the ideal of their oppressors, the servants that of their masters. One loves what one desires but does not have. Blondness seems to have pleased Dante, although, or rather because, he was not blonde and because blondeness was the apparent ideal of the aristocracy and the court. His emperors were blonde. Thus he could praise Manfred:

> *Biondo era e bello e di gentile aspetto*

> (Blonde he was, beautiful, and of noble
> aspect—*Purgatorio,* III, 107)

A man finds beautiful the woman whom he desires; whose exterior mirrors that psyche, that being, which he regards as ideal. A "dressy doll" will not please a man who has a "motherly" ideal; a man who appreciates "spirituality" in woman will not for long be attracted by a chubby, peasant woman. The ideal of beauty shifts, however; it not only oscillates according to periods and races, but even among individuals; it is bound to moods and age; according to the circumstances of life, the average person will be allured at one time by one, then again by another, type. Despite this, the types persist because they inexorably reproduce themselves at their place of abode. Thus if people from the South had a blond ideal of beauty, they nevertheless remained brunet; their ideal could not be realized in their country.

Now, however, there is an average female ideal, a type which again and again cuts its way through: beyond the disguises in vogue, beyond the taste of the period, the type of a healthy-looking woman with the typical face of a child is felt to be beautiful—a woman with facial features which reproduce the non-individual type of a child's looks. The "childlike"—both the psychically and the physically childish—is considered as beautiful (esthetically positive); it is felt to be "ingenuous" and graceful. Man loves "childhood": it is his yearning, and he loves its mental ambience and its physical looks; he always strives for the return to his pristine "dawn." The face of childhood is an "expression" of that wished-for world. In a majority of cases a child does not look ugly if it is not sickly, pale, or disfigured, and therefore "unchildlike." But a woman appears beautiful when she in some way embodies non-individual childhood—proportions that mean "harmoniousness" (this is, in fact, the "average visage" of the race and its average proportions), and when she exhibits the childlike face which is felt to be an expression of a childlike heart, the childlike complexion, and "attitude."

If this type, which actually is only a standard, is distorted by individual characteristics and furrowed by peculiarities—all of which destroy the illusion of childhood—then one calls such a woman at most "interesting," but not beautiful. For the judgment of esthetic pleasure derived from the human form, the mathematical ideal of harmony is of even more limited worth than otherwise. Esthetically speaking, traces of age in the female body are a blemish (rouge and powder are expected to restore the youthful face) although the body and the features of the face can preserve "conformity to law" until advanced old age. It is true that even the skin becomes "irregular" and uneven; the factor of youth and childhood is missing. This expected "comformity to law" is basically the average child-face of a race. But if the youthful-childhood aspect is lacking in a woman, she no longer, as a "plastic form," expresses the ideal of the human mind and is not considered "desirable" (at least as long as the feeling-life of the onlooker does not become "morbid").

To be added as the second factor making for esthetic feeling is the social factor already mentioned. The type of man developed in the leading classes of society is considered esthetically valuable as regards facial expression, stature, and physique. Social valuation engenders positive feelings and esthetic appreciation.

It is important for the comprehension of positive esthetic experience to account for the behavior of the psyche when it chances upon the ugly. The aroused feeling could be best described by the term disgust, but especially by "disillusionment." The onlooker in question would cling to the spot that evokes his aversion as if he were seeking for something. In his mind he constructs that form which he anticipates in its place. He feels: "This spot is wrong and it annoys me." Thus he restores the imperfect object into the wished-for image, into the ideal image he expects. In seeing mutilations by war, artificial limbs, and generally the crippled or the disabled (a missing nose, broken or missing or gold-covered teeth, and so forth), one can easily observe the "disillusionment," "the clinging to . . . ," and the reconstructive attitude of the mind mentioned above. One says that gold is beautiful, but not in one's mouth: one "expects" white teeth instead.

The sense of pleasure which arises in a person as he sees the beauties of nature contains the same elements which make up the sense of pleasure with regard to the "poetic." It is also pleasure produced by the circumstance that unrelieved emotional material has achieved its "expression"—that is, its "representation"—in an object of the external world.

There is, first, the pleasure of sight and of form corresponding to the pleasure in the rhythmical—a pleasure achieved from the sight of "the formed," the grouped, the "harmonious." That which is grouped in space constitutes the static condition of that "order" and harmony which vibrates dynamically in the rhythm of words and tones. As the world of objects generally is "shaped," "grouped," and thus brought into a "form," it becomes "clear" for our consciousness—that is, it is arranged distinctly and "meaningfully"; it thereby attains an aggregate condition which is accessible, manageable, and appropriate to the psyche of an organic being; the integration of this material of the world of objects into the system of consciousness is thus rendered possible, and the goal, a sleeplike languor, is reached. For the sake of this quiescence the psyche seeks after the formed and the clear. It desires the rest and the clarity which lead to rest.

In the second place, the world of objects is a world of symbols for the mind, of things, which, comparable to words, express the contents of the soul. Through this expression a part of the unrelieved psychic content finds a material frame for itself, as it were, in the world of outer objects; it realizes itself so that in them an inner liberation follows. The psyche thirsty for expression was unburdened and relieved through these symbols. The degree and intensity of this liberation depends on the expressive power of those objects of the external world. They must be not only the expression (representation) of some kind of feeling and thought—this they always are—but also the expression precisely of those complexes of feeling and thought which fill the psyche and absorb it to the brim. Now, they are released by those objects, and the mind is pacified after its oppressive contents were untied and, streaming forth, have found their embodiment in those objects. These complexes of interest and feeling have first stepped out of their *clair-obscur* into consciousness, have objectivized themselves into symbolic objects, so that the allayed mind may change over into the condition of sleep.

But if these expressive objects are not merely the expression of unrelieved tied-up material and hence not merely the implementation of a formal wish, but that of a material desire, an ideal of the mind, and if its appearance means happiness—that is, real wish-fulfillment—if they were longed for and anticipated, as happens at the appearance of the desired feminine ideal—then the esthetic pleasure occurring at the appearance of that object becomes most vivid. If the "desired" sexual object appears, then esthetic satisfaction is at its culmination. In that object a large part of the mind will find a "prop," expression, and redemption; many mental contents and psychic energies will stream forth, in order to find the object of deliverance, the most important symbolic object, in this erotic object.

When this happens, the mind falls back into a state of great contentment, which indeed may constitute the maximum amount of serenity attainable in life. This, the casting off of all disturbing psychic material, the attainment of a condition of tranquillity in consciousness, of a state of quasi-sleep, is the main object of psychic endeavor. The entire activity of the mind aims to achieve it; to reach it is the purpose of our mental organization. But this will become sufficiently clear when, not only poetic thinking, which is subservient to this urge, but the remaining activity of thought is analyzed; this must be the object of a separate inquiry.

Max Rieser resides in New York City and is a well known contributor to various journals both in the U.S.A. and Europe dealing with esthetic and philosophical matters. He was educated in Krakow, Poland and the University of Vienna, where he received his Ph.D. in 1920. He is the author of *The Psychology of Ivan Pavlov,* published in German in Munich, Germany and *The Philosophy of Paul Tillich,* published in German in Frankfurt.

This manuscript was edited by Robert H. Tennenhouse. The book was designed by Peter Nothstein. The type face for the text is Linotype Granjon designed under the supervision of George W. Jones and based on a face originally cut by Claude Garamond; and the display face is Bembo originally designed by Francesco Griffo in the 15th century for Aldus Manutius.

The book is printed on S. D. Warren's Olde Style Antique paper and bound in Columbia Mills' Bayside Vellum over boards. Manufactured in the United States of America.